Pink Triangles and
Rainbow Dreams

Pink Triangles and Rainbow Dreams

Essays about Being Gay in the Real World

John Arthur Maddux, Ed.D.

An imprint of C & M Online Media
Raleigh, North Carolina

Published by **Boson Books**

ISBN 1-932482-46-6 (print edition)
ISBN 1-932482-47-4 (ebook edition)

An imprint of **C&M Online Media Inc.**

C&M Online Media Inc.
Tel: (919) 233-8164
Fax: (919) 233-8578

Design by The Source: Mark Henry and Dan Maurice
Back cover photography: Aaron Kunkel

www.bosonbooks.com

This book is dedicated to

Michael Chanak and Matt Robinson,
without whom this never would have been possible

May the stars guide you,
Your dreams sustain you,
And life make it real.

Table of Contents

Introduction

This book is intended for all people: Gay, lesbian, bisexual, transgender, and non-gay. The focus in the book is obviously from the perspective of a gay man—how could it be otherwise when written by a gay man—but many of the essays include discussions pertinent not only to gay men, but to lesbians, and the non-gay population. Most of the essays are specifically directed toward a gay male audience; since, after all, that is the experiential background and understanding of the author. Nevertheless, everyone can benefit from reading the essays in this book; they have been written with the Gay/Lesbian/Bisexual/Transgender Community (hereafter referred to as the G/L/B/T community) and the majority community in mind. I am convinced that people of differing sexual orientations have the same hopes, fears, dreams, and desires.

The book is divided into three sections: On Being Gay, On Being Out, Open, and Politically Correct, and On Being Gay in the Real World. Section I: On Being Gay focuses on what it means to be gay, the kinds of discrimination we face in our daily lives, and how we react to issues of inequality, discrimination and bigotry (even within our own community). Section II: On Being Out, Open, and Politically Correct is directed towards contemporary issues within the G/L/B/T community, but can be read and appreciated by non-gays readers, as well. Section III:

On Being Gay in The Real World focuses more on issues that affect queers living in the real world and who are constantly struggling for equality. Hopefully, the humor that permeates the book will not be lost on any readers.

My hope is that by reading this book the G/L/B/T community and all non-gay people will come to better understand not only the issues of discrimination and inequality that face gays and lesbians from day to day, but will shed light on some of the issues within the G/L/B/T community that have been hotly debated for the past several decades.

My apologies to bisexuals, and transgendered people: I do not attempt to speak for you, or about you. I have included the breadth of the G/L/B/T community in many of these essays because I am an unapologetic believer in equality and that includes all of us, who, unfortunately, have not always had the best working relationships. Indeed, discrimination and distrust exist even within groups of people who supposedly share so much in common. Still, I am convinced that most of the essays in this book address issues common to all people who identify themselves as part of the G/L/B/T community.

Many of the essays in this book originally were written as editorial commentary on "Alternating Currents," a gay and lesbian radio program on WAIF-FM radio in Cincinnati, Ohio. Others appeared as commentary from a column I wrote for *Nouveau*, a regional G/L/B/T newspaper in the Ohio, Indiana, and Kentucky tri-state area. Still others were delivered as speeches at various rallies, fund-raisers, and Pride events. Most of the essays have been rewritten, updated, and edited to reflect a more contemporary view of gay issues.

There will be, undoubtedly, some people who will become offended by some of the topics and issues discussed in this book. I have diligently attempted to address a wide-ranging audience, but to speak to people of divergent ideologies, sexual orientations, and political and theological sensibilities becomes nearly impossible—it is difficult to identify a specific audience when discussing subjects that are as monumental as many of these are. My intent is not to assume that every gay man, every lesbian, every bisexual, every transgendered person, or every heterosexual share similar feelings, emotions, or sensibilities. I believe that if a reader is offended by some of the issues dealt with in this book, then that person should look more deeply into his or her mind and soul to examine the prejudices that might cause dismay.

Before continuing with the essays, a word about the title. Most gays and lesbians and probably a good percentage of heterosexuals understand the significance of the pink triangle—it has become known world-wide as one of the primary symbols of the G/L/B/T liberation movement. The pink triangle as a symbol in the G/L/B/T community stems from its use by Hitler's Nazis in World War II. Just as the yellow Star of David was used to identify Jews in Germany and other Nazi occupied territories, the pink triangle was sewn onto the clothes of homosexuals sent to concentration camps before and during World War II. In the 1970s it was unofficially adopted by gays and lesbians as a symbol of liberation, rather than the oppression experienced in Nazi Germany, and continues as one of the two most recognizable symbols of the gay struggle for equality.

The rainbow flag, another symbol of the G/L/B/T liberation movement was first designed for the San Francisco gay pride parade by Gilbert Baker in 1978. The original flag was made of eight colors: red, orange, yellow, green, turquoise, indigo, violet, and pink. Today, the freedom flag is composed of six stripes chosen from the following colors: red (life), orange (healing), yellow (sun), green (nature), blue (art), violet (spirit), indigo (harmony), and pink (sexuality). The flag has become flown world-wide and is recognized by the International congress of Flag Makers as the official flag of the gay liberation movement.

Using both symbols in the title of this book captures the political history of gays (dating from the holocaust and attempted extermination of homosexuals in Nazi Germany) and extending to the open culture of queerdom that typifies much of the twenty-first century world. The essays in this text discuss the fears, hopes, and dreams of gays, lesbians, bisexuals, and transgendered people everywhere; thus, Pink Triangles and Rainbow Dreams.

Read this book with an open mind. You never know what you might learn, or re-learn, from a new perspective. But most of all,

John A. Maddux

have fun! Learning should always be fun; when it ceases to be so, our search for truth will be in vain. If any of us—gay, lesbian, bisexual, transgendered, or non-gay fails to listen to reason and candor, then our hope for social, environmental, and political evolution will certainly be thwarted and we will become no better than our ancestors who lived in intellectual darkness, surrounded by myth, legend and fear.

Section One:
On Being Gay

One
Coming Out Is Essential

I don't know how many times in the past few years someone has called my attention to a gay-slanderous editorial in a newspaper, a homophobic joke on the radio, the heterosexist rhetoric of a politician, or the negative and condescending stereotyping of gays and lesbians on television or in the movies. Of course we now have Will and Grace and an increasing number of queer and dyke characters on television—even though such characters perpetuate homosexual stereotypes and sexless queerdom.

Often, when people see or hear something homophobic in the news or entertainment media, they demand action from one of the G/L/B/T organizations that try desperately to counter such pejorative stigmatization. Usually local and national groups respond by writing letters, meeting with alleged offenders, threatening boycotts, picketing businesses, and lobbying legislators. Sometimes their actions meet with success. If someone were to record the number of times offensive comments or stereotypes appeared in the news or entertainment media, we could probably fill a score of file drawers—there seems to be no dearth of slanderous, homophobic humor and news, even during a time of supposed enlightenment.

There are several avenues of recourse open to the G/L/B/T community to counter heterosexism in the media, but the fact of the matter is, we can continue spinning our wheels, fighting joke by joke, story by story, and character by character and get nowhere fast. Or we can go the media one better and declare war on homophobia by coming out of our closets, standing up for what we know is right, and being counted for who and what we are.

Ignorant people will always criticize and attack what they do not understand, especially when fear and misunderstanding are deeply rooted in religious myth and social taboo. This ignorance is perpetuated by three attitudes: a fear of the unknown, the stubborn adherence to ethnocentric mythology, and the repudiation of cultures, ideas, or values different from theirs.

Consider racial prejudice as an example of ignorance. African Americans have long been feared and misunderstood by the prevailing white power center because of skin color. Dark pigmentation has been historically (and incorrectly) linked to lower intelligence, and it wasn't that long ago that white scientists wrongly argued that blacks had smaller brains, and therefore, were less gifted and less capable of educated reasoning. For the most part, African Americans are still considered intellectually, economically, and socially inferior to Caucasians, and since they are physically different from the Anglo-Saxon homogeneity of American society, they must be inferior (as the argument goes). Thus, attempts to perpetuate white superiority have met with considerable success. The same can be applied to any other minority that has fought for liberation in this society: women, Native Americans, Latinos, religious groups, and various national and ethnic minorities.

Such can also be said for being gay. Gays and lesbians have long been unknown, ignored, and misunderstood by the majority of heterosexuals simply because of our love for persons of the same sex. We have been rejected by many Christian church organizations with their so-called Biblical prohibitions against same-sex orientation (even to the point of being persecuted, prosecuted, and executed in the name of God). We are most certainly different from the cultural norm of heterosexuality (thus, the fear, hatred, and prejudice we experience). And we are rejected because our social mythology does not adhere to conventional Americana. Accordingly, the majority of society feels justified in endorsing the silent approval of media and entertainment slander.

Because we are considered different we are open to attack; not only because of the reasons discussed above, but also because we seem too few in number to be taken seriously. Most minority struggles do not result in success until a significant percentage of that minority rises up to demand equality.

Consider again any of the various minority liberation movements that have taken root in the latter half of twentieth century America. Be they African American, women's rights, Native American, or specifically ethnic or religious, the opposing media slander did not end as a result of legislation or executive order. It ended because sufficient numbers of minority persons stood up for themselves and their rights, rendering media slander socially unacceptable.

The absence of media slander against African Americans and women is not because of legislation alone, a newly discovered sense of morality, or humanitarian acceptance on the part of the prevailing majority—it is simply the result of numbers. Pure and simple numbers that warn society that enough members of a particular minority not only represent people with the same hopes, dreams, and fears of the prevailing majority, but represent numbers large enough to translate into significant dollars, which in turn translate into serious consequences for business. The G/L/B/T has made its numbers known also. For example, the G/L/B/T community brought pressure to bear on Coors Beer, Disney Enterprises, and The Cracker Barrel restaurant chain, causing a complete turnaround in their homophobic policies. In fact, economic indicators project that in 2007 gays and lesbians will spend twenty-one billion dollars in the United States alone. Again, numbers translate into money.

The capitalistic ethic that argues money makes the world go round ironically ends up benefiting some minorities in their struggle for equality. Women and African Americans are earning a little more money and gaining a little more equality these days, but that is not so with all minorities. Native Americans are earning less money and Native Americans are making fewer inroads towards equality. Consider how even in the twenty-first century proponents still argue for using Native American names

as sports team mascots, claiming absurdly that the custom
honors Native Americans and is part of sports history. As for
those minorities that do achieve a bit more equality, it soon
becomes unacceptable to make racial, ethnic, or gender slurs and
misrepresentations in the media.

The lesson here is that we as a community must come out:
vocally, physically, and spiritually. As long as there are just the
few fighting for the many, no one—politician, religious leader,
housewife, or corporate executive—will believe that there are as
many of us as there are. Only when society realizes that we are
their teachers, ministers, bankers, truck drivers, plumbers,
politicians, and ball players will we begin to win the battle, and
only then will protective legislation be more easily enacted. It is
sad, but true, commentary that human rights mean little, that
financial opportunities dominate—and that in economic battle,
the conquering general utilizes all weapons.

Coming out of the closet means verbally acknowledging our
homosexual orientation to those who immediately surround us
and are important to us. It means telling our parents and
siblings, our closest friends, and the other people whom we
identify as being significant parts of our lives. Of course, each
one of us has to decide who among our sphere of influence needs
to know—no one can determine that for us. Coming out means
facing yourself, acknowledging your sexual identity, and living
your life in the open air of singularity; therefore, ending a life of
duplicity and lies.

Coming out isn't easy. By coming out we risk our families,
our friends, our jobs, our homes, our economic security, and our
safety. But staying in the closet is far worse, psychologically and
emotionally for the individual, and for the community as a whole

Coming out means figuratively shouting from the rooftops
that you're queer, and realizing that every day for the rest of
your life you will have to come out again and again and again
every time you meet someone new; every time you become
involved in a new situation. It means facing the reality that the
process of coming out is one that will last a lifetime—it isn't a
simple decision that is implemented one day and then forgotten
about the next. Coming out means living your life honestly from
that point forward.

Coming out is unique to people in the G/L/B/T community; for the most part the rest of the world doesn't know us for who we truly are. We don't necessarily look, walk, talk, or dress gay; unlike most minorities we aren't easy to identify. We can tell an African American, a Hispanic, and a Middle Easterner by the color of skin. Obviously we know the differences between a male and a female. But for gays and lesbians, there simply are not any distinctive physical, psychological, or emotional characteristics that indicate our sexual orientation.

I've been asked by sincerely interested heterosexuals what's the big deal, why do you have to come out, what's so important about announcing your sexual orientation to the world? We don't! Can't you just be quiet about it and still be who you are? As far as heterosexuals not having to announce their sexual orientation; well, of course not. The overwhelming percentage of the world's population is heterosexual; why should straight people have to announce anything about their sexuality?

We must answer no, we cannot be quiet about our sexual orientation when we are discriminated against and lack the same civil rights that heterosexuals do. No, we can't be quiet about it when we continue to be harassed, beaten, and verbally abused! No, we can't be quiet about it when we are denied jobs, housing, and equal opportunity. No, we cannot be quiet about it when we continue to be the butt of jokes that are still socially acceptable. Why should we be quiet? Why shouldn't we be proud of who and what we are? Coming out doesn't mean providing people with every detail about your sexual life, individual interests, or personal proclivities—such is information to be shared only by the most intimate of friends; the entire world should not be privy to such information. That is neither appropriate nor necessary. But it does mean being honest to the rest of the world politically, intellectually, socially, and personally.

The decision to come out is certainly an individual choice; however, I wonder when we will cease being ashamed of ourselves and accept that we are valuable and equal members of this (or any) society. Is it time to guilt the closeted? Perhaps. Shall we endorse the practice of outing the innocent, a political practice that forces closeted gays or lesbians—especially those of celebrity status—out into the open without their knowledge or consent? Certainly there are arguments in its favor. Does our struggle demand individual bravery and self-sacrifice? Absolutely. The success of any minority liberation movement is built upon the backs of those who sacrificed for the common good.

Coming out as a gay man, lesbian, bisexual, or transgendered individual means far more than conveniently slipping in and out of the closet for a Friday night visit to the bar, and then slithering back into the closet before sun-up Monday morning. Coming out means more than attending a once-a-year black tie dinner, then returning home for another twelve months of secrecy. Coming out means more than paying lip service to the cause of liberation and the honor of self-dignity. Coming out means more than anonymously writing letters to the defenders of homophobia. Coming out means more than playing at being gay or lesbian, then steadfastly denying (by word or silence) our sexuality to family, friends, and employers. Coming out means more than simply casting a secret ballot for a sympathetic politician.

We can continue writing letters to offensive radio stations. We can keep boycotting offending businesses until there is nothing left to buy. We can persist in fussing and fuming until we turn lavender in the face, or we can take a giant step toward personal integrity, communal pride, and universal equality by taking that one step out of the closet, accepting who we are, and demanding that the nonsense we call responsible journalism and entertainment cease its heterosexist war against each and every one of us.

Two
Loving Yourself

When was the last time you said to yourself, I love you, you're a good person, and I want to do something nice for you today? I know it sounds silly, but it's not. Reminding yourself that you are a good person is perfectly OK. In fact, it's advisable because it is critical to sound mental, physical, emotional, and spiritual health—and for us gays and lesbians, it's absolutely essential.

Being gay or lesbian can be tough. We are constantly reminded about how different we are and sometimes we tend to let it get us down. It's difficult enough for gay adults to adjust to the prejudice in a heterosexist society, but remember back to when you were young and things really seemed out of control? Remember those unhappy days of living in the closet; knowing who and what you were, but being afraid of admitting, even to yourself, the most horrible secret imaginable—that you were a queer or a dyke?

It wasn't easy growing up gay or lesbian. Homosexuality was shrouded in prejudice, myth, and misunderstanding:

The church claimed it was a sin

The government said it was illegal

Our parents usually ignored the whole subject

The schools banished information about homosexuality from the curriculum

Hollywood and television portrayed gays and lesbians as swishy fems, butch dykes, and scandalous n'er-do-wells
Our playmates told fag jokes—and we told fag jokes—and we died a little more inside each time we laughed, knowing full well that, all the while, we were ridiculing ourselves.
Everything we heard or saw about homosexuality was linked to negative images; there wasn't anything positive about being queer—it wasn't the All-American way to be.

When we got to the age of reasoning, our whole life began to revolve around proving that we weren't really queer; proving it not only to ourselves, but to the people who, we were certain, knew our terrible little secret. Remember how we tried so desperately to be heterosexual: those cumbersome dates; the awkward locker-room talk about that hot person of the opposite sex; the hours spent trying to become aroused by the *Playboy* (or *Playgirl*) centerfolds; the denial that one of our friends stimulated sexual desire; the feigned attraction to the most sensual female or male model of the day?

No, it really wasn't so good, but we made do the best we could, knowing—or rather hoping and praying—that some day we'd outgrow that horrible curse that caused us to be aroused at the thought and sight of someone of our own gender. But hoping didn't work, and after a while, praying seemed just a waste of time—after all, the church had convinced us that God wasn't on our side, even though we, too, had been created in Her image.

We over-compensated and tried desperately to make up for the evil we thought lurked within our souls; and sometimes, if only for a moment, we ended up thinking that we really weren't as wicked as we thought; after all, how could we be, we were...well, we were US! So, we tried to be better, more polite, more successful, more lovable, and more all around good than we actually were. We tried desperately to be the best little girl or boy in the world, and sometimes it worked. Everyone said what wonderful, well-behaved children we were, but we knew the dirty, ugly truth that kept us from being like everyone else. We knew that we were attracted to people of our own sex and, my God, we even wanted to touch them, to feel them, and maybe—dare we dream—to kiss one of them!

Remember? Those early years of recognition weren't very much fun, but we endured, grew up, and passed through adolescence into adulthood, still with our secret locked safely inside.

Then it happened! Suddenly, almost overnight—wearied by the years of self-hatred and doubt—we changed; and we were never to be the same again. No longer could we stand the duplicity of perpetuating a double life. No longer could we tolerate the hypocrisy of living in the closet. No longer could we worry about how we walked, or talked, or acted, or how we stole a glance at the man or woman next to us in the check out line at the grocery store. So we came out—some of us openly and without hesitation, some of us only to ourselves, but our truth could never be hidden again and for the first time in our lives we felt free: totally and absolutely, free.

Even in our freedom, there were still those uncomfortable moments, those times when even at our most secure, the long forgotten, negative images of being queer crept back into our consciousness like a deeply repressed link to our past, and reminded us that, in fact, we were not like everyone else. We were part of an invisible minority and still misunderstood and despised by much of the world's population.

Now, in our present, with personal acceptance achieved, sometimes we still end up, if only for a fleeting moment, feeling a little depressed, a bit distanced from the world around us, and we dislike ourselves again and begin to feel ill-at-ease with who and what we are.

It's not unusual, it's not hypocritical, and it's not our fault. It happens to every gay man and lesbian at one time or another. After all, being homosexual means constantly living with the realization that we are not like the majority of the world. Being homosexual means invariably fighting for our souls. Being homosexual means undoing all those years of forced, negative conditioning. Being homosexual means countering everything that was imprinted in our minds at an early age. But during our times of deepest despair, it is critical to remember that we are good people, we are equal to anyone else, and we are entitled to live life as fully and with as much pleasure as we can.

So, be good to yourself, for a change. Take a long look in a mirror, sometime soon, and say to yourself: "I love you. You are a good person. I want to do something nice for you, today." And the nicest thing you can do is to love yourself completely and without hesitation as a gay man, a lesbian, a bisexual, or transgendered person. It is important, it's necessary, and it's fun, because believe me, WE ARE WORTH IT!

Three
The Beauty Trap

Beauty is in the eye of the beholder, or at least so the saying goes. These comforting words of wisdom are easily accepted by the beautiful, suspiciously regarded by the average, and outright rejected by those who regard their appearance as something less than attractive.

It's not easy believing tired and worn clichés, especially for those of us not overly blessed in the looks department. We want to believe them—we really do. We boost ourselves with personal reinforcement every time we look into a mirror, but somehow, we always fall back into the self-defeating abyss of believing the reflection of our negative qualities, rather than of our positive.

Well, we groan, I'm just not attractive enough. I'm too fat, too thin, too short, too tall, or too—anything else. My nose is too big, my muscles too puny, my body too much out of shape. Every day the negative conditioning of the beauty trap ensnares us and it never seems to end. Everywhere we look we're bombarded with beautiful-people-advertising that seems to do little more than reinforce our poor self-image—and we end up believing the worst about our physical selves.

It can be argued that beauty is a learned attitude of social behavior, rather than individual physical acceptance, but I'd like to meet the person who really believes that. Think about it: what other reason is there for the billions of dollars we Americans spend every year on beauty treatments, cosmetics, weight clinics, plastic surgery, home exercise equipment, and health spas? Sure, we can diet, pump iron, work out, do aerobics, and sweat our pounds away, but in the end there is nothing we can do about the physical characteristics with which we were born and that make us the unique individuals we are.

We're raised hearing that beauty is in the eye of the beholder and that beauty is only skin deep, but everything we see and hear tells us otherwise.

Consider the effects of Madison Avenue propaganda. In magazines and newspapers, on television and in the movies, on billboards and posters, we see beautiful women, handsome men, big muscles, artificially enhanced breasts, and washboard abdomens. Day after day we are flooded with so much anatomical perfection that it doesn't take us long to start comparing our own body unfavorably to the beauty that is paraded before us in a never-ending physical Nirvana.

But what is even more discouraging is that too many of us in the gay community have assimilated the whole marketing scam lock, stock, and barrel. We esteem beauty, we worship at the alter of the well endowed hunk[1], we pay homage to physical perfection, and we end up perpetuating our own perceived inadequacies as though they were undeniably real.

Ironically, the curious part of the beauty trap is that we gays like to think of ourselves as having been liberated from the more traditional conventions (and expectations) of society. We purport that our minority status makes us that much less affected by the whole body-beautiful bilge of marketing-mad America. But we really haven't liberated ourselves from the beauty trap mania. On the one hand, we're quick to reject the aspects of society with which we don't agree, while on the other hand, we embrace the physical as though it were a god.

Visit any typical gay bar on a Friday night, listen to the conversation, watch the cruising, and observe who's hitting upon whom. Our hostelries are loud with language that betrays our so-called liberation. The atmosphere is ripe with exposed pectorals, bulging crotches, and perfectly sculpted muscles. The bar management hosts strip shows, beauty contests, and the best chest, body, or crotch competition. The whole hedonistic scene negates individuality and emphasizes that which gay liberation supposedly rejects.

Take a look at the magazines and videos that cater to the gay male community (most of which are owned by heterosexuals who understand where their bread is buttered). They are loaded with gorgeous hunks, rippling muscles, and dicks so enormous that they make any normal man feel grossly inadequate—and we love it! We scarf up every imaginable type of porn magazine (depicting hunks, studs[2], daddies[3], bears[4], or twinks[5]) that perpetuates the definition of what male beauty should be, and witlessly turn into size queens, pec lovers, abs aficionados, and buns babies. And in course, we end up hating our own bodies because they don't mirror the Adonis on the cover of the latest hot-stud magazine.

Look at the comics in the magazines for gay males. They're ripe with bulging baskets and well-defined butts. We've turned any number of overly accentuated cartoons and grotesquely drawn characters into a subculture of desirable phenomena that we actually believe, and yet the comics cater to the stereotypes that surround homosexuality and enable the myth of physical vanity that haunts the gay male community.

Thumb through the personal ads of any gay newspaper. For the most part, they emphasize the physical and ignore the intellectual and they make us wonder why everyone else is so gorgeous and we're so...average!

Scan the Internet, check out the personal profiles created by chat room addicts and the looking-for-love web sites, and you'll discover that a significant percentage of the physical information being passed off as truth is exaggerated fantasy. Although one could argue that playing games of I'm-a-Handsome-Hunk on-line is harmless, it continues to propagate the concepts of beautiful bodies, desired youth, and abnormal penis size.

But it's a sham, a sad comment on the way we live and the liberation we like to think we've achieved. Only about five percent of the population could comfortably fit into the category of beautiful. Another five percent, unfortunately fits into the category of unattractive, and that leaves the rest of us ninety percent who are average, normal looking guys. So what can we do? Continue buying into the nonsense that causes self-defeat, depression, and constant body-parts-comparison, or shall we truly liberate and accept ourselves for who we are, regardless of muscles, abdomens, and groins?

It would be far better to love ourselves for who we are, not for what we have or do not have beneath the jeans. Let's emphasize our attractive qualities and resolve to not give a damn about fantasy expectations.

Anyone can accept himself, physically, for who he is. I know I've given it a go, and if I can do it, anyone can. After all, my body isn't exactly what I'd like it to be. I don't pump iron and never will. My nose is larger than I'd prefer. My hair is receding. My muscles are...well, more like vague, undefined areas of my body, than they are chiseled beef. And I'm in big trouble if anybody judges me on penis size.

So, maybe my looks are just average, but so what! Long ago I accepted that *Playgirl* will never come knocking on my door for a centerfold spread, and I doubt if anyone will become mesmerized when I enter a room. But I've learned to like myself for who I am—not who I would like to be—and that translates into acceptance, acceptance translates into attitude, and attitude translates into beauty. That's all there is to it. It really is that easy.

I know you're sitting there, right now, thinking: Right, this guy can't even see me, how does he know what I look like? You're absolutely correct, I don't have any idea what your physical imperfections might be. I'll bet anything that you possess a number of positive qualities. I'll bet there are lots of terrific points in your favor. I'll even bet that there are far more attractive aspects to your appearance than you'd guess. Of course, it's up to you to accept the truth and discover just how beautiful you really are. And when you do, look out! There will be no turning back, because beauty belongs to everyone, and believe me—everyone can be beautiful.

Four
Husband Hunting

I don't know how many times in the past few years I've had conversations with different gay men about finding a husband, or at the very least, getting a boyfriend. It seems to be the one most often shared concerns of the gay male community. Searching for that perfect man consumes our time and energy and seems to dominate every waking minute of our day. Our singular, most popular activity seems to be the great sport of husband hunting.

Conversation frequently revolves around the fact that many gays can't seem to find that one special person to fulfill the all-encompassing role of the other half, or worse—that some of us might never find that person (a powerful desire with which we were so ingrained growing up in heterosexist America)! Living as a single man does not portend an especially positive view of self-identity, but then, certainly being unattached is more realistic than living in a fantasy of one-night stands, mornings after, and dashed hopes.

When you think about it, there are relatively few permanent relationships among gay men, although the numbers are ever increasing as more gays become individually aware and are able to give as well as to receive. In fact, to a certain extent, permanence seems antithetical to being gay. We are constantly searching for that perfect companion from a seemingly endless string of prospects, but seldom hit pay dirt. We compare ourselves against the few, apparently, ideal gay relationships that exist, and end up feeling worse about ourselves than necessary. We feel unloved, unwanted, unattractive, and un-everything else, and ask ourselves why. Why him and not me? What's wrong with me? Why can't I find the same happiness he's found? So we torture ourselves with self-recrimination until we've thoroughly convinced ourselves that we just don't deserve a relationship and never will.

Get over it! Perhaps we won't find that perfect man with whom to grow old and crotchety; maybe we won't gaze into the sunset of our years together from our rocking chairs of tedium. Life doesn't always work out the way we hope, but there is a lot more to life than coupling (despite what society would have us believe). Besides, being in a relationship isn't critical to our health or happiness (again, despite what we've been led to believe).

We live full, valued, and exciting lives as single men. Single doesn't mean being alone and lonely, as heretical as that might sound. Face it guys, we've bought into the Judaic-Christian, movie theater, music industry nonsense of you're nobody until somebody loves you, lock, stock, and perfect-bodied barrel, and we punish ourselves for not having the things in life that other people have (in this case a companion).

Whether or not we meet that one special guy begs the question. Reality, ultimately, focuses upon what we do with, and how much we enjoy life as it is—not as we would like it to be, or as we dream it to be—and our happiness is not defined through mutual dependence upon another person. Life truly is nothing more, and nothing less, than what we make of it, and for some culturally perpetuated reason (parenting and the procreation of the species?) we think that if we don't have that one significant person-mate in our life, that we've been dealt a lousy hand of cards, and that life will be little more than an endless continuum of loneliness and pain.

Of course, there are legitimate reasons why relationships are so difficult to maintain in the gay community. First of all, there aren't as many of us as there are of them (non-gays), so the pool from which to draw is significantly reduced. We make up only between ten and fifteen percent of the population (depending upon who's numbers you believe), and that greatly lowers the chance of meeting someone with whom we might fall in love.

Then, to further complicate the numbers game, only about fifty percent (or less), of the gay twelve to fifteen percent is open and comfortably queer. That further reduces the available number of possible partners to a very small percentage of the gay population—not a very promising size from which to find the perfect mate.

But even if numbers weren't a nemesis, there's the question of compatibility. We assume that just because another person is gay, that we'll automatically get along. What a joke! Coupling with someone demands more than a romp in the hay, more than a hunky body, and more than sexual desire. Simply because two people are queer doesn't mean they will share the same interests, values, ethics, politics, hobbies, and philosophies. Compatibility demands not only romantic passion, but sensitivity, caring, shared interests, common philosophy, and a sociopolitical understanding that affords comfort and agreement. Unfortunately, too often, we close our eyes to the love available right in front of us because of a dozen reasons why we can't fall for a guy who doesn't fit our image of type or age—and we lose out on one heck of a lot of potential.

Too many gay men fall into the candy-store, one-after-another boyfriend syndrome; frantically moving from one man to another in a frenzied attempt to find Mr. Right. Frequently, we allow ourselves to become sexually intimate with our dates even before actually learning anything about them—other than physical attraction. We fall in and out of love so quickly that it's hard to keep track of who and when we dated, and we become disillusioned and miserable when we discover incompatible differences with that supposedly perfect lover (desperation is the bane of happiness).We often forget that anyone, given the right equipment, can have sex and that just about anyone can share physical intimacy with another person. However, not everyone we meet will be compatible, loving, or emotionally satisfying. We lose sight of the fact that compatibility and love are the characteristics at the heart of any lasting relationship, and instead we focus on physical appearance and sexual pleasure.

To further complicate the problem of finding the right guy is the way we've been raised in Western culture. Men have been conditioned to be aggressive and competitive with one another, traits not easily addressed in a lasting relationship. We tend to challenge our lovers, rather than nurture; compete, rather than complement; argue, rather than compromise; attack, rather than negotiate; and criticize, rather than cultivate. In other words, in too many instances, we just don't know how to love.

Undoubtedly, it is difficult to maintain any type of permanent relationship in this day and age. Consider the statistics for heterosexuals: divorce rates continue to spiral upward, spousal abuse is rampant, career goals are frequently at odds and disruptive to marriage, and couples are more willing to call it quits because of perceived differences, rather than working them out. And it's similar in the gay community. No wonder—given the other variables of gay life—that gay men have difficulty maintaining permanent relationships.

Even if the numbers were not stacked against us, even if we were able to find another man comfortable with his homosexuality, and even if we were able to discover compatibility with that one special guy and overcome the problems common to all relationships (gay or straight), it wouldn't, and shouldn't, define who we are. No one can enter a healthy relationship, until healthy and comfortable with himself, no one can love another person, until learning to love himself, and no one can share the togetherness necessary to a companionship as long as he intends to compete and demand.

It isn't falling in love that should be paramount to our happiness. It isn't finding that one special person that should complete our existence, and it isn't coupling, just for the sake of coupling that should define who we are. It is *us*—each and every one of us as individuals who should establish the parameters of personal success.

If we truly can learn to love ourselves, if we can learn to enjoy the friends we have, if we can draw sustenance from the things that make us happy and that bring us joy, then we've truly discovered the secret of happiness. Only then (and not through, nor because of another person) will we learn to be fulfilled, worthwhile, comfortable, or happy.

If, then, we are lucky enough to find that one special person, that one guy who seems to make life a bit more interesting, then great! But if, for some reason we do not—so be it! Life will continue, and so to will we. So, let's get on with it and live.

Five
How to Make It Work

We live in an age of disposable relationships—not only in the gay community, but in the non-gay community as well. In the heterosexual world the divorce rate continues to rise and in the gay community we seem to have a penchant for relationship jumping; that is, going from one love affair to another with little regard for commitment or permanence. Maybe it's just a temporary phenomenon (for both gays and non-gays). Perhaps it's because we're too impatient waiting for that right person to come along. Maybe it's because we place so much emphasis on genital sexuality. Perhaps it's the result of not having the appropriate social conditioning and role modeling with which to identify.

When considering the throwaway mentality of modern society, it appears that only a handful of men in our community understand that which goes into making a successful relationship. It's a question most of us have considered at one time or another—especially at that point when we're considering making a commitment to another person—but it's a question we somehow expect magically to take care of itself, like learning to walk.

But learning to walk is a lot easier, it comes naturally. Loving another man is more difficult in a society disposed to exclusive heterosexuality; we are provided no direction in learning how to be with a person of the same gender.

Many gay men consider a relationship simply the reflection of heterosexual marriage; that was the model with which we were raised and that is how we expect to actualize our partnerships. Those who regard gay unions in such a manner, mirror the conventionality of a non-gay partnership by adopting conventions that mimic heterosexuality: exchanging marital vows, using partner identified terminology, and functioning in a fashion that reflects the expectations of non-gay society. That's not necessarily bad, but it's not realistic either, because being gay is non-traditional to begin with and attempting to parrot relationships that have been established for economic and religious purposes begs the question.

Historically, heterosexual marriage served the purposes of legitimizing procreation, establishing a functional economic unit, providing care for the extended family, legalizing inheritance, and creating an environment conducive to the rearing of children. Initially, the purpose of marriage was to establish familial units that were responsible to the larger community and which formed the basis of communal living and the development of village life—institutions strictly for the promulgation of the culture and the continuity of tribal autonomy.

Theologically, the purpose of marriage was to legitimize sleeping together (i.e., sex) under the mythological approval of human and God, to insure clerical control over all aspects of the couple's life, to promulgate specific religious populations, and to provide money for the church's coffers.

Economically, marriage was intended for the purpose of procreation in order to provide for human capital and to assure male inheritance. Despite what we have been led to believe, the concept of romantic love is a contemporary phenomenon in terms of humankind's evolution. Up until the nineteenth and twentieth centuries, romantic love was a privilege of the aristocracy, not the common person.

Few gay unions adhere to such traditional conventions. Men do not procreate with men (although gay men are adopting and raising children in ever increasing numbers), and our unions are inherently non-conventional, so there exists little need to adhere to societal expectations and cultural norms. Economically, most of us have not become co-conspirators in perpetuating the great human capital scam (again, there are always exceptions to the rule—consider the Log Cabin Society!). Why then, do we insist upon replicating a heterosexual union when non-tradition is the bottom line of gay life? Granted, marital benefits and civil unions have even become the focal point of the twenty-first century gay liberation movement, but dare those issues compare with the need for equality and political liberation?

A problem common to many gay relationships is that, in many cases, they are taken too lightly (certainly, that is common to many heterosexual relationships, as well). Too many gays enter a commitment with the idea that when the first problem develops, it's easy to jump ship. We seem more inclined to spring from relationship to relationship like Mexican jumping beans, exchanging relationships like unwanted birthday presents and forgetting commitments as quickly as we do yesterday's news. Little is accomplished save pain, loneliness, isolation, and perpetuating the stereotype of homosexual promiscuity.

Another issue problematic to gay relationships concerns the amount of excess cultural baggage unintentionally carried into a union by unsuspecting gay men. Gay men have been culturally and socially programmed with internalized negative attitudes about themselves. We have enough problems learning how to love ourselves, let alone learning how to love a person of the same sex. In too many cases, we lack the necessary learning patterns denied us by frightened and confused parents who would rather reject our sexuality than accept it and teach us. We suffer from low self-esteem and from more than our share of self-hatred. It's not easy trying to nurture a relationship with another man, when we have difficulty taking care of ourselves. It's tricky trying to break the learning patterns ingrained by a society that rejects individuality. Men are conditioned to aggressively compete with one another; not to exchange love. The negative stigma that we carry into our relationships causes too many problems—even without intention or conscious deliberation.

Another problem common to many gay relationships is that there exists in our community an inordinate emphasis on genital sexuality. Again, because of negative cultural stigmatization and conditioning, we have been forced into acting out our need for intimacy in ways that emphasize eroticism. We are forced into denying our orientation, our needs, and our interests from the very first day we discover our sexuality. Consequently, our emphasis on sexual gratification becomes paramount, even to the neglect and exclusion of intimacy and affection. We are quick to settle for orgasm rather than intimacy, gratification rather than affection, and a quick one-night stand rather than lasting tenderness. The problems are many and not necessarily caused by the individual, but all is not hopeless. Many gays have established successful unions; we need only look to them as role models.

To begin with, gay men, despite negative social conditioning, share the same needs, the same desires, and the same dreams as do our heterosexual friends. We want only to love, to have security, to share companionship, and to experience a sense of belonging, intimacy, affection, and tenderness—the needs so eloquently detailed by Maslow's[6] psychosocial hierarchy. Those needs might be realized in ways different from our heterosexual counterparts, but in the everyday world, there exists little difference in what we want except that we want it with someone of the same sex.

A successful gay relationship is possible. We need not despair and think only in terms of quickies, one-nighters, and a lifetime of loneliness. It might not be easy to redefine the programming that has been foisted upon us, but it is possible. Certainly, it will necessitate the same amount of work and effort that goes into successful non-gay relationships—probably even more, given the cultural dimensions involved. We need only take time to care about our lover, to compromise when necessary, to nurture and be sensitive, to respect, to be honest and open, and to love. That is what makes for a successful relationship. It has nothing to do with one shallow affair after another. There is nothing magical or mystical about it. It simply takes a lot of hard work, tenderness, compassion, understanding, and most of all *love*.

Six
So Who Is That Person Next to You?

Until recently, I had never given serious thought to what term was appropriate in describing a loving gay or lesbian relationship. In the past, I used the currently fashionable term, lover, but now that I've given it more thought, I think a more inclusive term is called for.

It's so much easier for non-gay couples to come up with terms to describe their relationships; after all, heterosexual unions have been around for centuries and everyone understands the terminology used: A man's legal partner is his wife, a woman's legal partner is her husband, and a single person has either a girl (woman) friend, a boy (man) friend, a fiancé, or a fiancée. The terms are descriptive, well defined, and culturally understood.

In the gay community it's not quite that simple. Since gay/lesbian liberation is a recent (and still expanding) phenomenon, we haven't a history of linguistic tradition with which to provide description for our more intimate affairs. Most of the possibilities just don't seem suitable. For the most part they sound silly and contrived, and so we plod along stumbling over ambiguous phrases like Pirandello's[7] characters in search of an author.

Consider the possibilities: The term most commonly used to describe a committed, loving relationship between two gays is the word, *lover*. At first, lover seems acceptable. It's accurate, pleasant, and descriptive. Or is it? According to Webster's, a lover is: "A person who is in love with someone else." Fine, I can buy that. Further, Webster's concludes that a lover is "A person involved in a non-marital, sexual relationship," but that's not acceptable. For gays and lesbians it's pejorative and discriminatory, and therein lies the problem.

The term *lover* carries a one-dimensional connotation of sexuality and although sex is certainly an important part of any romantic relationship, Webster's definition does injustice to the depth and breadth of caring and intimacy. The word *non-marital* need not be problematic since gays recognize the sanctity of their own relationships (especially since, increasingly, we are being denied civil union and marriage rights in state after state). Despite what society and religion might think, a gay relationship involves more than merely sexual intimacy. The term lover doesn't comprehensively describe the full extent of a gay relationship. To most non-gays (and even to many gays) the term lover connotes sexuality only and thus is not descriptively inclusive of the entirety of a gay relationship. Strike one on the term lover.

Another term frequently used in describing a gay couple is the word *partner*. This term should be shelved immediately; it's obtuse and non-descriptive. Would you seriously refer to your lover as your partner? It's sterile, emotionless, and reeks of market-place mentality. Imagine someone saying: Hi, I'm John, and this is my partner, Rick. Your partner in what: Crime? Business? Tennis doubles? A duet? No thanks; partner evokes images of a business arrangement, a legal contract, or something out of the old west. Businesses have partners. Corporations have partners. Cowboys have partners. Older people who marry for companionship have partners. But gays and lesbians shouldn't have partners—at least not in the intimate sense. The term is too barren; too legalistic. Strike two on the term partner.

A third term used to describe gay relationships is the unsightly word *companion*. Ugh! The mere thought of it makes me gag. Talk about emotionless and sterile. Companion sounds like a 1890s spinster aunt traveling arrangement: Henrietta and her aunt were traveling companions throughout Europe last summer. Sorry, but companion suggests neither commitment, nor love. It's like two old friends spending their last days together. There is too much distance with this word, too many overtones of friendship only. Companions are compatriots, buddies, best friends, or pals. People who share practical living accommodations are companions, but two people sharing the same bed are not. Strike three.

Well, then, what about the terms *boyfriend* and *girlfriend*? Please, you've got to be kidding. The terms boyfriend and girlfriend hardly reflect the maturity of a serious relationship. They might be descriptive, and yes, they do convey the nature of a relationship such that everyone might understand what it is, and certainly, they communicate the idea of love and caring, but, the terms sound far too high schoolish. Fifteen-year-olds have boyfriends. Seniors in high school have girlfriends. Forty-year-old-men and women do not. Merely substituting the words man and woman for boy and girl is even worse. Robert is my man-friend—what the heck does that mean? Sounds like something out of a nineteenth century British novel. Think how the term boy/girl friend would sound at sixty-five. Pretty scary, huh? No thanks, this one won't do either—there has got to be something better. Strike four (I'm using pre-twentieth century baseball rules).

A fifth term occasionally used in describing a gay relationship is that of *life-mate*. Good gracious, no! I don't want a life-mate, thank you. It sounds like a relationship described on the Animal Planet network. Lions have life-mates. Gorilla's have life-mates. Canadian Geese have life-mates. The only humans I know who have life-mates are either yuppies or clinical psychologists; not normal people. Would you seriously introduce your lover as your life-mate at a social gathering? People would rightfully wonder what planet you're from. Besides, what would that make a couple's children: life-lings, life-spring, life-litter? No, I'm sorry, the term life-mate is too clinical and too silly, and definitely won't work. That's strike five (now I'm beyond the rules of baseball).

We're almost out of possibilities; only a few pathetic phrases remain. How about the frightening phrase *significant other*?

Now there's a really scary term. Sounds like something Adler[8] or Jung[9] would have thought up.

Hi, this is Tony, my significant other. You're significant other what: friend, sex-buddy, tailor, interior decorator—what? The term is far too confusing and suggests you have another significant other somewhere else, or that everyone else in your life is insignificant. Think about it! The word other means "in addition to" or "being the remaining one." Thus, if Tony is your significant other, then you must have another lover somewhere who is your significant other lover, or would your other significant other lover be an insignificant lover in contrast to your first significant other? Forget it; sounds too much like, she sells seashells down by the seashore. The term is awkward and confusing and had to have been coined by someone whose life was void of any significant others—anywhere. Strike six (you've been called out on strikes long ago).

That brings us to *special friend*. How cute; how closet-case protectionist. Spare me. I can just hear the conversation now: Hi, this is my special friend, Steve. Um-hum, sure he is, and just how special is Steve? Special friend is what you say to protect dear old Aunt Clara from finding out that you're queer. Special friend is how you describe the person you're bringing to the office picnic. Special friend is how you introduce your bedmate to your minister. Special friend is the term your relatives use to explain Steve to the youngsters in the family. But you don't tell your friends, or your peers, or other queers that your lover is your special friend. If you do, then you are cheating yourself and lying to those whom you supposedly trust. Anyway, the people closest to you already know the truth—whether you want to admit it or not. They can see through your facade. They know what a special friend really is, so you're not fooling anyone except yourself. The term should be discarded as quickly as possible. Special friends penetrate nothing more than your thoughts and feelings. Strike seven (geeze, you've been out for a long time now!).

Finally, we come to the terms husband and wife. I hear them being used more and more in the gay community. In fact, they've almost replaced lover as the acceptable terms of choice. Well, excuse my insolence, but my lover is not my husband, we are not heterosexual, and there is little we can, nor want to do to successfully imitate heterosexual tradition and marriage. The terms husband and wife have specific definitions within the context of anthropological, opposite sex coupling and presuppose a set of traditionally defined familial expectations that are realized within the constraints of heterosexuality. Certainly, gays and lesbians have evolved extended families, but members of the same sex are not husbands, nor are they wives. I suppose the terms are acceptable if duplication of heterosexuality is the goal, but the gay community has long attempted to define its own set of values and ideals. Why then, should we adopt phraseology that defines us in terms of the culture that serves as our oppressor? I say, ditch these terms right away.

In fact, ditch them all—they are all confusing, non-descriptive, and pedestrian. I'd rather come up with a new phrase to describe my lover-partner-companion-boyfriend-life-mate-significant-other-husband. I'm not sure what it might be, but I'm working on it. If you come up with any ideas let me know.

Meanwhile, if you see me on the street, hand in hand with another man, don't expect any fancy terminology to describe the extent of our relationship. When I introduce him, by name, rather than as a possession, accept who he is and figure out the rest of the puzzle for yourself. People enjoy the challenge of second-guessing, anyway, so why not give them something significant to chew on?

Seven

They Say That Breaking Up Is Hard to Do

Breaking up is painful; ending a relationship can be one of the most devastating experiences in life. It temporarily renders everything meaningless during that time between initial loss and inevitable recovery. It makes the world seem more hostile, our lives seemingly pointless, and a job not so important. At one time or another, we all experience the pain of breaking up, and although it is one of life's realities that we'd rather do without, the fact is, if we expect to experience love, we should also be prepared to experience the pain of lost love. It's an inevitable scenario oft repeated from the time we first discover the exhilaration of intimacy, to the last time we're moved by the excitement of romance.

But, we seem to have a penchant for turning breaking up into an ugly experience that results in damaged egos, wounded pride, and shattered dreams. Breaking up is hard enough without purposefully trying to destroy the other person. Too often, the ending of a relationship disintegrates into name-calling and argumentation. We're quick to point an accusing finger at one another, we expect friends to take sides, we dispute mutually acquired property, and we conjure every insignificant polemic that develops during the relationship. Some of our actions are understandable—after all, breaking up can be devastating—but for the most part, we deal with the end of a relationship in ways that betray our normal sense of decency and disregard our maturity and intelligence.

Seldom do we enter a relationship believing it will end in separation. We don't expect to hurt the other person. We don't sit around thinking up ways to cause sorrow. We don't want to inflict pain. Relationships sour, they wither, they die. Sometimes, they're just not meant to be, and like it or not, love isn't always enough to save a relationship from disaster. Certainly, there are instances when deception and dishonesty are at the root of a failed relationship, but those are a horse of another color. For the most part, it's just a matter of things not working out, and even then, our natural inclination is to hurt the other person, to embarrass him, or to cause guilt. Such feelings are natural and serve as protection against our own pain. We get over it eventually—time does have a curious way of heeling all wounds—but in the meantime, we hurt like hell and want to get even with the focus of our pain.

First we want answers. Then we fight back. We boast idle threats. And finally we rationalize our misfortune and accept the inevitable. And so it goes. For a while, we feel like losers: another relationship down the drain, another teary-eyed chapter added to our book of lost love, another misfire that reinforces the belief that we'll never find that special person. We become bitter and angry, petty and spiteful, and withdraw into a world of resentment, disappointment, and self-doubt.

But it doesn't have to be that way. There was a time when we loved the person who caused our sorrow. We weren't forced; no one held a gun to our head. We entered the relationship knowing full well that things don't always work out, and we willingly accepted the good, knowing all along there was a possibility for the bad.

Obviously, it would be better to call upon our more mature characteristics to help soothe our wounded egos—those positive qualities that for a time made the relationship the realization of our dreams. It's always better to remember the good rather than the bad, but sometimes remembering things we can no longer have can be painful. Nevertheless, it makes for a more mature way of facing life, and it makes picking up and going on that much easier.

Most people who have gone through a break up would like to have had the opportunity to have brought the relationship full circle; to end it on a positive note similar to the one on which it began, but it is frequently impossible to accomplish that during times of emotional stress and personal involvement. It hurts too damn much! Then, after the person is gone, it's too late; nothing more can be said at that point.

Therefore, I'd like to propose an open letter to all the lovers of the world who have, at one time or another, been stung by the pain of unwanted separation. It goes like this:

Saying goodbye is hard. At least it is for me and I imagine it must be for you too. But, I'd like to think that this isn't as much goodbye, as it is "until we meet again," for I know that we will meet, again, someday. So let's accept, for now, that our love wasn't meant to be and go on from there—you, your way, and me, mine. I know that sounds simple, but it seems the only answer.

It was good, you know. You did a lot for me and I hope I did as much for you. There were just too many variables over which we had no control; I know it isn't a question of your not loving me and I know that I will always love you, but sometimes love just isn't enough and in our case, I think this will be best for both of us.

When I think back to how I felt when I first met you, I can remember how strongly I fought against falling in love. I was frightened and as vulnerable as a child, but after a while, I couldn't prevent the emotions from getting the better of me. I fell in love with you, and although knowing that I can't have what I want hurts, I am comforted in knowing that what we shared was truly love—even if only for a short time.

I want to say thanks for the love. Does that sound silly and self-effacing? Of course at this point, I don't care how it sounds. So, thanks for sharing, for being a part of me and with me. Thanks for trusting and respecting me, and for treating me like someone special.

When I first fell in love with you I thought it was simply because you brought enthusiasm to my life—a spark of excitement that reawakened me to spring. But now that I can look back with distance and understanding, I realize that even though it was all of that, there was so much more. You not only ignited that spark, but showed me that I really did want to love again—I won't ever forget that!

I can't pretend our break up doesn't hurt, because it does. There will be times when I'll miss you terribly, times when I'll want to be with you and want to gaze upon your face and enjoy your smile. There will be times when I'll want to listen to all those silly things you'd say and times when I'll want to hear you singing off-key in the shower. There will be times when I'll want to come home from work and tell you about my day, and times when I'll just want you to be near. I guess the worst part is knowing that I can never hold you again; that I can no longer kiss your lips, touch your face, or snuggle up against you or shield you from the hurt of a fickle world. I know that I must let go, because I do love you and I can't imagine being with you unless we could be the way we once were.

Know that our time together was good; I wouldn't trade it for the world. Know, also, that I will always be here for you—not as a one-time lover, but as the friend I have now become.

Should we drift apart, as former lovers often do, and pass into different worlds far removed from the one we shared, know that there will always be a special place in my heart; a place that no one else will ever fill. Once there was a time when I could look into your eyes and see the love and understanding you so unselfishly gave; now, I can only take consolation in knowing that I can look into my memory and see a Sunday afternoon in the park.

Farewell, my love—take care and remember to always smile.

Eight
What about Us in the Country?

Recently, I spent a weekend with friends in a small, rural town in central Ohio. It was one of the most enjoyable weekends I've spent in quite some time.

It was a comfortably rural kind of weekend, complete with meat and potato meals, pretzel and beer snacks, and an enjoyable blend of country-western and contemporary music. Missing were the typical dinners, wines, and evening liqueurs of A-gay[10] city culture (those upwardly mobile snobs of our community). There weren't any designer jeans, famous maker shirts, or Doc Martins to be seen anywhere. There was an abundance of flannel, denim, and cowboy boots; but they weren't being worn as bar costume, they were honest to goodness, everyday clothes—the kind worn by the men some of us city folk try so desperately to imitate (and very poorly, I might add).

Thankfully, our conversation avoided the use of gay-speak and queer-talk. There was an acceptable amount of camp spoken, but it seemed almost foreign to my friends' normal vocabulary, and was, I think, added only for my benefit, since I was one of those city queers! Done and said, it was a comfortable, homey weekend—and thank God there wasn't an A-gay to be seen for miles. Sadly, though, the weekend came to an end and I had to return home long before I was ready. Sadly, I say, not because the weekend failed to live up to my expectations—it did so, and more—but, sadly, because the closer I got to home, and the big city, the more distanced I became from rural America and that part of gay life we in the city so often forget, or worse, ignore.

I was returning to a job that afforded the freedom of being out of the closet: returning to the ten or so bright-city-light gay bars, returning to a myriad of gay and lesbian organizations that provide activity and support, returning to churches that minister to gay and lesbian worshipers, returning to the sheer numbers of gay population, and returning to the anonymity that permits a gay man or lesbian the choice of openness, conformity, or the closet. My friends, on the other hand, remained in Smalltown, Ohio, with its one too easily identified gay bar, and—well—its one too easily identified gay bar!

We talked that weekend about life in rural America and about their decision to stay in Smalltown and to share what they are certain will be a lifelong commitment. One friend teaches in an elementary school, the other runs a gasoline station. Neither has elected to come out because of a fear for his job. They are both religious, but can't attend church, together, because single men don't do that in their community. They don't dare let the neighbors in on their secret. They can't accompany each other to social functions or job-related events (without raising eyebrows after the second mutually attended activity). They can't show affection in public, there are no gay groups to join, no support, no socialization, no queer operated stores, restaurants, or bookshops, no one with whom to talk about being gay—only that one poor excuse, hole-in-the-wall gay bar.

They are aware that by living together they focus suspicion upon themselves, but they are willing to deal with the misgivings of their conservative community. As far as the townies are concerned, my friends are merely sharing expenses until the right women come along. Of course how long that frail perception lasts is anyone's guess!

Their choice mandates that they remain closeted and that they carefully protect their reality with intricate webs of deceit. They expressed regret about having to remain in the closet, about never being able to share their happiness with friends and family, about living lies, and about the difficulties of being gay in a small town. Some people argue that my friends' decision to stay in Smalltown is negotiable, that living in a provincial, heterosexually biased area that will cause nothing but headaches isn't worth the price they pay, and that they should move to the city. But that attitude seems more than a little condescending and much too big-city gay; not everyone is given to the rootless, nomadic character of contemporary American life. People who were not raised in rural America, with its binding ties to family and locale fail to understand the attachment to home and location, and besides, Smalltown is where my friends were born and raised, and Smalltown is where they choose to live and die. They don't want to move.

They want to surround themselves with nature; to become closer to the environment of which they are a part, and they believe that by moving away from life in a small town, they will lose something valuable—a part of themselves; the essence of who and what they are. But they have a long struggle ahead, a lot of loneliness, and more than enough isolation.

Why should they be forced into fleeing their home because of bigotry and prejudice? If such is the case for rurals, then how long will it be until all of us are forced into anonymity despite living in Big City, Anywhere? The thought of flight from oppression strikes me as defeatist, especially when considering the imposed plight of our rural gay counterparts. Too many of us in the cities don't seem to care about the problems of our brothers and sisters in the country, but our struggle for liberation should include everyone. We champion big city rights and cheer big city pride events, but forget about our friends who cannot share our feeling of liberation.

And oh how we forget! Oh how we ignore the plight of our small town, rural American brothers and sisters and speak in terms of New York, San Francisco, Chicago, and so on and so on, as if those cities truly were the great gay Meccas of freedom. But the larger cities do not create the boundaries for gay America, and they do not establish the precipice of gay culture, although the majority of gay/lesbian publications would have us believe as much.

We occasionally include the smaller of the big cities in our ethnocentric mentality, but as for places like Rural Route #2 or

PO Box 23A, forget it! They don't seem to exist as far as we're concerned, and yet we have the nerve to chant at our rallies and parades that we are everywhere!

So what about our friends in rural America? What options to they have?

Well, they could pack up and move to the big city and become another number in an endless sea of faces, but that's not good. They could burst out of the closet and face the ugly reality of lost jobs, lost friends, rejecting families, bigotry, ridicule, harassment, and violence—without a means of support and encouragement—but that's a horrible prospect. They could remain closeted, hiding like frightened victims of oppression— and that's unfortunate. They could keep their shades drawn, speak in euphemisms, practice deceit, fear discovery, ignore their needs, swallow their pride, and keep their doors locked— and that's terrible. Or they could just go on as they have been— closeted, frightened, and alone.

I'm back home now, content in the security of my big city house, big city friends, and big city lifestyle. I'm out and open and I know that can mean harassment and discrimination— sometimes even violence—and yet I'm somewhat protected by the sheer size and anonymity of my environment. Nevertheless, I can't stop thinking about my friends and the millions of other small town and rural gays and lesbians throughout America. How do they do it? Where do they go to socialize? With whom can they talk? For them, the geography of circumstance has effectively rendered their lifestyle untenable, which necessitates constantly fighting a battle for dignity itself.

It is our battle, also, and if we in the cities are serious about our demands for equal rights, then we must look beyond the selfish boundaries of Big City, Anywhere and remember the heartland of America. We are after all everywhere: On the farms, in the sticks, in the villages, in the towns, and in the cities. Those of us fortunate enough to benefit from the opportunities of big city living must eliminate the ethnocentricity of attitude and learn to think in terms of the universal community. We must accept the roles that have come to us by way of happenstance and carry the torch of liberation to our brothers and sisters isolated by geography. It is up to us to help extend the network of love and support far beyond the bright streets of the city and rekindle the flickering candles of hope for gays and lesbians in the shadows.

We are people little different from our small town brothers and sisters. We share the same hopes, the same dreams, and the same fears. We differ only because of geographical location. We are—like our non-big-city family—merely the products of environment, and we dare not insist (simply because of self-proclaimed sophistication) that we know what is best for people of varying locations. We might have access to more community money, better resources, more organizations, and the reality of sheer numbers, but we are not the guardians of community thought.

Most of all, we must care; not only about ourselves, but about gay men and lesbians everywhere. For if any one of us is not free, then surely none of us are free—and that is a tragedy of monumental proportion that we dare not tolerate.

Nine

The Second Wave

There was a time, not too long ago, when we gay men were feeling pretty good about ourselves as far as AIDS issues were concerned. It was the early 1990s and things seemed to be pretty much under control, at least as under control as a deadly disease can be.

There was a more comprehensive, although not completely adequate, response from the government. Laws were being passed protecting HIV-infected persons from discrimination, and the public was beginning to realize that HIV and AIDS were not God's wrath against gays, but rather, a viral disease that could be contracted by anyone—heterosexuals included.

More money was being spent for research into life prolongation, cures, and vaccines; more empathy was being extended to those who suffered the effects of AIDS; and the gay community seemingly had addressed the issue with intelligence, compassion, and understanding. Even though there were still far too many of our friends and family dying from AIDS, the rate of new infections among gay men had fallen markedly. The gay community had become the model for the country.

For the most part, we had closed our bathhouses, responsible voices in our community were speaking out loudly and harshly against promiscuous sex, and we focused on sexual responsibility and the numerous pleasurable opportunities associated with safer sex. We had seen ourselves dying, and we didn't like what we had witnessed. We seemed the champions of civility, compassion, and reality.

Then the bottom fell out. A second, unexpected wave of HIV infections, especially among younger gay men, began to rise. Since the mid-1990s, the rate of infections among younger gay men has increased at an alarming rate. When the disease was first identified in the early 1980s, we relied on the (now) tired excuse of well, we just didn't know. And that was true. The strange, cancer-like disease that seemed to be affecting gay men (particularly in this country), Haitians, and intravenous drug users spread like a forest fire of death and we could hardly blame ourselves, entirely. Who could have guessed that the loving act of sex could lead to something as devastating as HIV, prolonged suffering, or even death?

We were innocent in our ignorance. No one had yet identified what was happening, there weren't any studies to link the new disease with sexual activity, and the idea that physical intimacy could result in something other than a possible, occasional bout with a curable (or, at least, treatable) socially transmitted disease was unthinkable. But we soon learned to the contrary.

Thousands of gay men came down with the strange, new viral infection. Eventually, millions of gay men died of AIDS-related complications, and we began to get the message. But now, despite our knowledge, our education, the availability of free condoms, and the realization that a quick roll in the hay can lead to something other than a broken heart, we are (once again) becoming infected and suffering in increasing numbers. So what gives?

We're supposed to know that safer sex can prevent the transmission of HIV. We're supposed to understand that promiscuous sex is physically dangerous. We're supposed to accept that standard sexual practice includes the use of condoms and ingenious safer-sex practices. And yet the numbers of newly diagnosed HIV infection among gay men is on an alarming rise.

Why? Of course there are always the standard answers: It won't happen to me (right, and neither will paying taxes and having to face life's myriad of problems); I was in love (since when does love include ignoring your partner's well-being?); I was drunk (well, put down the bottle and use a little common sense!); He told me I was the only man for him (the only man among how many others?); We were being monogamous (evidently, not!); We'll all get it sooner or later (yes, I guess that's probably right, if we don't use intelligence when having sex); I've got low self-esteem (and becoming HIV+ will improve that?); and the most alarming of all, I'm too young—AIDS is an old man's disease.

Part of the gay community's campaign and education during the 1980s was to convince people that HIV and AIDS knew no barriers of orientation, race, gender, ethnicity, economics, or age—in short, everyone was susceptible. But that seems to be one for the ages, now.

AIDS workers throughout the country report the same findings over and over again. In counseling with young men newly diagnosed as having contracted the HIV virus, they hear the same comments, repeatedly: I didn't think it could happen to me; he was my age; gosh, he was only twenty-one!

When once we stood as a model of intelligence and restraint for the bulk of the general community, we now risk renewed discrimination, distrust, disrespect, and retribution. And all because we're too stubborn to exercise control, or to use a condom!

The incidents of HIV infection continues to climb in the non-homosexual community, especially among African American women and white, suburban teenagers, as well as the terrible plague destroying Africa and other parts of the developing world, but those are the people who generally have been left out of the AIDS education loop or whose parents and countries have turned their collective backs on reality.

Parents who campaign against sex and AIDS education programs in the classrooms are the same people who won't even talk to their children about sex! The illogical rationale suggests that they'd rather risk their child's death than have him or her exposed to intelligent, sensitive, and potentially life-saving education. Typical of such ignorant mentality are comments such as: my kid isn't going to have sex (yeah, right, and neither did you when you were a teenager), my son isn't going to hear about

condoms and intercourse from some queer teacher (so who's he
going to hear it from, some kid on the street?), and the
granddaddy of them all, I believe in abstinence (great idea,
although not very realistic).

In a recent study, an overwhelming percentage of young
people who took an oath swearing off sex until marriage reported
that they believed that any physical act of intimacy, short of
intercourse, is abstinence. They claimed that oral sex counts as
abstinence, and only traditional vaginal penetration counts as
sex. Any act of sexual intimacy, other than vaginal penetration
was OK and was not violating their oath of being abstinent! I
have great empathy for those who have become infected—
especially the uneducated—but little sympathy for the obstinacy
and right-wing hypocrisy of those who have fought reality all the
way! Rejecting sex education in favor of hoping that your child
will ignore the pressures of sex in an overly sexualized society
bodes of ignorance and stupidity.

But getting back to the G/L/B/T community—it's time we
reasserted our commitment to AIDS education, and that means
more money spent by our organizations, more time devoted to
learning about the issue, more emphasis on intelligent sex, more
information about how AIDS can be spread, and more insistence
upon safer sex practices, the use of condoms, and honest, non-
pejorative discussions about monogamy and promiscuity. And
therein lies part of the problem. As a community we recoil at the
suggestion that promiscuity is unacceptable. We continue to
make excuses for anonymous sex. We champion the bar culture
that promotes heavy drinking and physical intimacy. We spend
billions of dollars purchasing magazines and videos featuring
men with enormous dicks, but shallow, meaningless
relationships. We reject the possibility that we can get along
quite well for several weeks at a time without getting laid.

There will be those who read and criticize these ideas
because they demand honest consideration of our behavior. A
belief in monolithic thought (that is that we must all think, talk,
and respond the same) continues to exist in our community, so
we dare not criticize our own! I've heard the pathetic excuse that
these ideas don't account for the poor, unfortunate men who
can't get sex other than from an anonymous pick-up, because

they are too deeply hidden in the closet. Well, too bad, come on out—the sun shines much brighter on the reality side of life! I don't have a great deal of compassion for people who would rather risk their lives and the lives of others than accept the reality of whom they are. There is no good excuse for bending over for an unknown partner, simply because you're still in the closet and horny.

It is painful to still see friends dying of AIDS-related complications. It hurts to find out that a twenty-two-year-old has been diagnosed HIV positive. It is deeply saddening to understand the devastating potential this disease still holds for the G/L/B/T community, the individual, and the world.

But we can stop it!

No, we haven't, yet, found a vaccine to prevent HIV. No, we don't have answers to the myriad of AIDS-related problems and questions. No, we still haven't eradicated the disease that threatens our very survival. But we do know how to prevent it! We have the education available. There are thousands of dedicated, caring professionals who have committed their lives to working with AIDS-related programs, and we have safer-sex information at our disposal and condoms to use whenever the urge hits.

We need to get busy again, rededicating our efforts to ending this disease in our own community, as well as everywhere else. This is not just an old man's disease. Regardless of whether you're in love, or just lust, you can contract HIV! Let's stop mixing alcohol with sex, and let it be known that anonymous, promiscuous sex is not acceptable, responsible behavior. We can do it! All it takes is a little willpower and a condom.

If we don't react immediately, there will be another discussion like this one ten years down the road, addressing the same issues to a scattering of gay men, who by then will have dwindled to less than a fraction of the strong, vibrant community we are now. We are out of excuses—and, damn it, almost out of time!

Ten

The Garden

There once was an old man who tended a garden. It was a beautiful garden, and he, an intelligent and caring man. The garden was filled with zinnias, lantana, roses, dahlias, daisies, and more and was not only his pride and joy, but brightened the entire neighborhood in which he lived.

When neighbors passed by the old man's yard, they would say: Oh how lovely the garden looks this year. Isn't it more beautiful than last? Or they would sigh to themselves and say: How peaceful and serene it makes me feel. I think our neighbor has outdone himself this season.

Strangers to the neighborhood would stop and look, savor the wonderful aroma that came from his garden, and marvel at the rainbow colors that made his garden the talk of the town.

Seldom did anyone—neighbor or stranger—pass by without pausing to gaze upon the old man's garden; in fact, entire families would drive miles out of their way on shopping trips just to see the garden. Lovers picnicked outside his gate. Children frolicked in the peace of the grassy hillside above his yard. And old men and women spent hours sitting near his locale, contemplating the many years that had passed, and the few yet to come.

The old man's garden attracted admirers from miles around. The old man worked his garden for many years: rising each morning during the warm weather to weed, water, nurture, and prune; and staying each evening in the cold weather to till, clear, and prepare for the next spring. He was singularly given to caring for his garden; nothing else mattered to him. He had no other hobbies, no other interests, and no other diversions upon which to focus his passionate energy. His garden was his life, and his life was his garden.

And so it was that this old man, of singular interest, went about tending his garden year after passing year, regardless of summer storms, winter snow, or his frail health. Had you awakened early one morning and passed by his house, you could have seen him on his knees weeding and pruning, planting and cultivating, protecting and harvesting. Were you to pass by late in the afternoon you could see him sprinkling his botanical children after the hot, mid-day sun had settled near the horizon. And had you been sitting in your living room late on a summer's eve, you could have heard him whistling and humming as he gave last-of-the-day attention to his blossoming friends.

The old man and his garden become as one, and as the decades passed, everyone came to know him only as the old man with the garden. For years that came and went, everyone knew and expected that come each spring, after the snows had melted and the cold had eased into warmth, that the old man would be out tilling and planting and in a few weeks the first virgin stalks of life would appear and several days after that, the first buds would blossom. It was like a steady, uninterrupted clock of sunrise and sunset; life and death; the old man was always busy and his garden was forever beautiful.

But it came to pass that one day, early one morning, long before any of the neighbors had awakened, the old man with the garden was out doing his customary morning gardening when suddenly, and quite to his surprise, he came across a single flower that he had never before seen in his garden.

From where did this come, he wondered in amazement, this flower of unequaled beauty! It was large, perhaps twice the size, or more, of his most prized zinnia; and wide, at least half again the width of his champion dahlia; and beautiful, more beautiful than all the roses and cannas and the hundred score other flowers that his garden bore.It was tinted purple near the edges of the blossom, and shaded into different hues of lavender and pink as the gentle pedals edged close to the stamen and pistols. Around the outside of the blossom were six star-shaped green leaves—a green that made the deepest wetland grasses pale in comparison. And it grew from a stalk of downy moss that was as soft as a newborn's cheek.

The old man with the garden dropped to his knees and marveled at the beauty of this unusual flower. He became more captivated by this one blossom than by any he had ever seen...or with his entire garden, for that matter. And he decided what he must do.

No one must see this flower, he whispered to himself. It is a special flower that has grown in my garden for reasons I do not yet understand. I will take it into my house and care for it alone—away from the prying eyes of neighbors and strangers; away from the jealousy of the other flowers. And with that thought, the old man dug up his new and beautiful friend, transplanted it into a fresh clay pot, and took it into his house.

There he remained with his special flower, night and day, day and night, pausing only to eat and sleep; forgetting to tend the needs of the garden in his yard. The old man became obsessed by that one flower and regarded it only for the beauty it possessed. He did not think about from where it had come. He did not wonder how it had grown alone, among the other flowers. He did not regard it for anything other than its beauty. He simply admired it, loved it, and ignored the beautiful garden that for so long had been his devotion.

After a few weeks had elapsed, passersby began to wonder and to whisper among themselves. Where is the old man? We haven't seen him weeding in the morning, or watering in the late afternoon.

And what has become of his garden? It is wilting, fading, surely it will soon die. But no one called on the old man; he was left to himself, his admirers believing that everything would be all right and that in another day or two—perhaps more, but certainly not very much longer—the old man would emerge and tend to his fading garden. But he did not. He stayed in his house, alone, with his new flower and forgot about his garden, his neighbors, and the strangers who passed by wanting to catch a glimpse of the most beautiful garden in that region. Little by little, day by day, flower by flower, the beautiful garden began to die.

Many weeks thereafter, long after the old man had first found his beautiful flower, he awoke one morning—and as so many times before—looked to the northerly window where he kept the clay pot, and cried aloud.

The special, beautiful flower that for ten weeks had provided the old man with singular happiness was lying limp across the dirt of the clay pot: faded, spotted, and dead.

In his grief for the passing of his special flower, the old man with the garden thought long about what could have caused its death, when suddenly it came to him. He rushed to the calendar, checked the month and date—which he had not done for many weeks—and discovered, to his dismay, that summer had passed and his beautiful flower was nothing more than an annual expression of the season and had succumbed to a natural death with the passing of summer into fall.

For several moments the old man remained silent, unable to consider anything but the death of his beautiful flower. His sadness was great, his resolve, broken, his joy, shattered. But then, remembering the beauty that his other flowers provided, he rushed to the window to behold the garden he had ignored for so many months, but to his horror—it was too late.

In place where once had been a cacophony of color and beauty, was nothing more than wilted stems and withered stalks. No flowers blanketed the hillside of his yard. No beauty glistened in the morning sun. No life grew from the hard, brown earth that had once radiated with abundance.

He moved from the window and sat in despair. He had nothing, now: no beautiful, singular flower in a pot inside his house; no garden; no neighbors and strangers passing by, waving in admiration; no hobby to occupy his time. He was alone in his house and his world—alone with nothing but death and isolation.

And he wept.

Should you awaken early one morning, and pass by the old man's house on your way to anywhere, you will not see him out tending his garden. If, late one afternoon, you should chance to walk the path that leads to his door, you will not hear him humming as he waters and prunes. And if you should be sitting in your living room on a lonely summer eve, you will not hear the old man with the garden thumping about as he prepares for the next spring. Rather, if you listen carefully in the silent darkness of the passing summer, you will hear him weeping softly to himself, as he has for the many years since his garden first died. He is weeping for the loss of that one flower, weeping for the death of his beautiful garden, weeping with a loneliness that penetrates the depths of his soul.

Neighbors no longer pass by the old man's house in admiration of his beautiful garden. Strangers no longer come from miles around to catch a glimpse of his radiant, rainbow blend. Lovers no longer picnic outside his gate, basking in the romance of his botanical delight. Children no longer play on the hillside above his yard.

The neighborhood is now silent, except for the hushed sound of an old man weeping. People come and go about their business, as they always did, and always will, but, now, with much less happiness and considerably less joy. The sun rises and sets, as it has done for millions of years, and will do so for millions more yet to come—but there is no beauty to behold beneath its lonely rays that shadow a barren garden where once life thrived. The old man and his garden have been consumed.

Section Two:
On Being Out, Open and Politically Correct

Eleven
I Try to Be Politically Correct

Being gay or lesbian and living openly as a part of the gay community necessitates an acceptance of important social regulations with which we must all abide. One of the most critical aspects of being gay concerns the manner by which we conduct ourselves, or being politically correct as it is more idiomatically referred, but given the quickness with which political correctness changes from week to week, it is, at times, impossible to adhere to proper decorum. So what's a person to do?

I've found a little known and infrequently used book that addresses the concerns of being politically correct and other questions concerning etiquette in the gay community. Being the public servant that I am, I share with you the secrets of leading a proper and politically correct life. Here, then, are but a few of the more valuable tips from the *PC Manners Guide to Homosexuality and Being Politically Correct*:

A male homosexual must adopt a persona that contradicts his natural behavior; any guise will do. Some choices include: offending women by the use of a drag personality, dressing in leather and chaps, country-western attire, or wannabe-wigger apparel (but only for bars and cruising purposes), affecting attitude that suggests superiority to all other gay men, or dressing in only the most fleeting of contemporary fashions.

Male homosexuals should use pejorative language describing women only when cloistered with other gay men. At all other times they should pay lip service to women and pretend that they are sensitive to women's issues.

A male homosexual can be referred to as a she when being referenced by other gay males for the purpose of public subterfuge, or when enacting campy behavior.

A male homosexual is a gay man or a queer—not a homo, a fag, or a gay boy. There do exist variations of gayness within the community that indicate the exact domain to which a gay man belongs; however, the terms twink, chicken[11], chicken-hawk[12], sugar daddy, or dowager[13] should be used only by the initiated, or by those who are of that domain.

Bar flies, sugar daddies, twinks, bears, chicken hawks, and dowagers must not affiliate with members of opposite groups. Physical attraction to other men must be maintained within one's specific subculture. Crossover relationships are not advisable; in fact, if such should occur the offender will be barred permanently from his dominant domain.

A female homosexual should be called a lesbian or a gay woman, not a dyke—unless, of course, one is a dyke, or knows a dyke intimately. In that case it is acceptable to use the term with permission. Use it only in the company of your most intimate friends, or while in the presence of a dyke; and make certain that the dyke to whom you are referring is not a lesbian separatist.

A lesbian separatist is a woman who believes in creating exclusive space for women and who prefers not to associate with men, or even consider the possibility of male value. Such women believe that men have ruined the world and singularly personify violence, domination, and oppression. A politically correct gay person accepts the lesbian separatist (or any other separatist faction for that matter), regardless of the nature of its bigotry.

God is a She, not a He, and Adam was a he, not a she. However, Eve was not really a she, but rather a he in drag; thus proving (much to the chagrin of Christian fundamentalists) that God really did create Adam and Steve.

A queen is a flamboyant gay man, but a king is not a butch lesbian. A king is a heterosexual male (except in the most notable cases of Louis XVI and George III). If a queen objects to the term, refer to that individual as a Lady-In-Waiting.

Heterosexuals are properly referenced as non-gays. The sexist slur *breeder* may be indiscriminately used by gays in private conversations, or in public at parades, rallies, and demonstrations. The fact that the gay community objects to pejorative name-calling by non-gays, should in no way mitigate the use of the term breeder; double standards are perfectly acceptable while being politically correct.

Gays and lesbians must be registered with a politically correct, liberal party such as the Democratic or Green Parties. Gay men and lesbians can be Republicans only if they promise to remain hidden in a closet. Under no circumstance should a gay or lesbian Republican permit anyone to know of his or her political affiliation (with the notable exception of the vocal and frighteningly dangerous, Log Cabin Society). It is common knowledge that no gay man or lesbian could be politically conservative.

Gays and lesbians are expected to support gun control, pro-choice, affirmative action, minority quota hiring, the anti-nuclear movement, Green Peace, Amnesty International, universal health care, male strip shows, celebrity drag queen mud wrestling, and all self-described progressive causes.

Gays and lesbians should only vote for political candidates endorsed by gay community organizations. If other types of organizations endorse other candidates, the gay voter should not be confused, but should understand that only his or her preferable organization knows what it is doing and what is best for the community—and vote accordingly.

If you are a gay man, you should not enjoy contact sports—particularly football, basketball, or hockey. You may however, engage in team sports such as volleyball, soccer, and bowling as long as you don't care about winning.

If you are a lesbian, you are permitted to enjoy contact sports—especially football, basketball, and hockey. You may also engage in other team sports such as volleyball and softball, as long as you allow yourself to become obsessed with winning.

Gay men may not host Super Bowl parties, unless the gathering involves conversation and gossip that have nothing to do with football. If a gay man, at such a party, were to react to the game, cheer for a touchdown, or otherwise function in a manner that suggests interest in the sporting contest, he should be politely excused from the festivities. Lesbians, however, may host Super Bowl parties, at which the women in attendance may overtly react to the game itself.

If you are an upwardly mobile gay man, you should prefer wine over beer, cheese over chips, and canapés over tacos and salsa. You should be prepared to cook exotic soufflés, work out at the club, pump iron, and enjoy aerobics. It is considered impolite to gain weight, loose your hair, or otherwise appear human.

All gays and lesbians must belong to at least three national gay rights organizations to which they pay inflated dues and from which they receive little, other than semi-annual newsletters and weekly requests for additional contributions.

Gay men should not move in with a lover until at least two months after first contact, lest such a situation cramp cruising and one-night stands. Additionally, gay male unions must accept the concept of open relationships, three-ways, and lustful cruising.

Lesbians are permitted to establish joint living arrangements prior to the end of a first date, but must remain monogamous throughout the duration of said experience.

Gay men would be wise to hide their affinity for science fiction, B grade horror flicks, and Arnold Schwarzenegger movies. They are better off worshiping Betty Davis, Bette Midler, Barbara Streisand, Marilyn Monroe, Judy Garland, Elizabeth Taylor, Madonna, Cyndi Lauper, Janet Jackson, and Britney Spears (although no one can actually understand why).

Gay men must accept that size does matter and not consider a date with a man of average, or—dare it even be said—below average penis size. Admissions to the contrary betray the myth that all queers are at least two inches in length above the average size dick. Lesbians, however, may date women of any breast, waist, or hip dimensions.

Lesbians may not subscribe to any magazines in which women are portrayed as sexual objects. Gay men, however, should subscribe to at least two magazines that present genitals and penises as exaggerated extensions of King Kong.

All gays and lesbians are expected to attend at least fifteen fund raisers per year—four of which must be held at the same time in different locations—and five of which must be at a cost of at least $75.00 or more per person.

Gay men and lesbians may not dispute the late hour during which fundraisers are held. They are expected to accept the premise that gay people either do no work, or have late afternoon retail sales positions.

And finally,

Gay men are expected to function on Gay Standard Time, even when specific activities begin two hours beyond the advertised time—punctuality will not be tolerated. Lesbians, however, may be optionally punctual.

These are only a few, simple, easily adopted rules of politically correct behavior. Remember, it is essential that no matter whom you are, what you believe, or how you regard your own philosophy, you must not function as an individual at the expense of monolithic thought. Do not attempt to be unique! These rules have been established for the purpose of bonding the community as one. They have been implemented to encourage uniformity and to guarantee appropriate behavior. Thus, the gay community can more comfortably mimic the institutions and regulations that have kept us oppressed. To blend is to liberate!

Just do as you are told by your community leaders and do not question the reasons for, or the consequences, thereof—after all, anything else would be politically incorrect.

Twelve
It's Time We Grew Up

Nobody likes to be criticized. Few people enjoy hearing negative comments about themselves, and none of us are especially enamored by suggestions that we should change our more unacceptable characteristics of personality. But we do know that, ultimately, the only way to grow, the only way to become a better, more efficient, and more productive human being is to listen to unfavorable criticism, learn from it, and work on changing those aspects of personality that less than flatter our public personae. The same can be said about the gay community. We might not like hearing the less than favorable comments about community behavior—it certainly isn't very pleasant—but it is time our community accepted reality and grew up!

We humans accept that responsibility and logic are a developmental process of maturation. We don't expect a ten-year-old to think and reason as would an adult, we excuse teenagers for what we consider their lack of responsibility, and we understand that young people don't have the experiential skills for dealing with life's inconsistencies.

Nevertheless, there comes a time when we do expect that the adolescent, the teenager, and the young adult listen, learn, grow, and blossom into what we hope becomes a contributing member of society. We adults don't cotton to the irresponsibility of people who drink and drug themselves into oblivion, rather than face life as it is—warts, problems, happiness, and all. We become disgusted with the grown-up who prefers thinking and acting infantile, rather than acting with the rationality of adulthood. And we don't tolerate the caprice of individuals who would rather ignore reality in order to play in their world of make-believe. We don't like it. It doesn't work. We can't accept childish behavior in adulthood.

Why, then, would we be willing to accept the immaturity of the gay community? We (the gay community) have been around for nearly five decades in our most recent incarnation as a liberation movement, but we seem content to accept our less than attractive side and allow our young to learn also from those of us who act the fool.

We silently watch as our youth (and still too many of our elders) trick themselves into AIDS, drink themselves into waste, and deny the reality of who they should be as individuals and as a community.

We perpetuate the bar culture by luring younger gays into a skewed picture of what gay life is all about: bars, liquor, blowjobs, and one-night stands.

We focus upon sex and a fuck-me mentality by pandering pornography as an idealized representation of "real life gay," all the while creating a false image of what a gay man or a lesbian should, or should not be.

We emphasize the body beautiful by lauding physical perfection as if it were the definitive explanation of what a gay man should truly look like (and oh how miserably most of us fail imitating that one!).

We continue our petty, high school mentality by encouraging rumor mongering, backstabbing, and organizational one-upmanship as being the "norms" of gay sensibility and politics.

We do all those things we so harshly criticize heterosexual men for doing (but we do it with the same gender so I guess that makes it acceptable!): we loudly and verbally cruise in public places; we ascribe individual worth based on physical appearance; we treat each other like sex objects; and we focus upon the physical rather than upon the emotional, the intellectual, and the spiritual.

I've been around long enough to see the results perpetuated by our ignorance, and we've all experienced the fallout of our immaturity. We've seen our friends become HIV infected and die, when education and prevention are so readily available. We've all comforted friends who are in the depths of another depression because that one-night stand didn't turn out as expected. We've heard the self-depreciation that comes with thinking that we're less than desirable because no one hit on us at the bar last night. And we participate in backstabbing and rumormongering against people and groups we really don't truly know.

We have yet to deal with the problem of sex in the parks and in public rest rooms; and yet, rather than speaking firmly against it (be it gay, straight, closeted, or bisexual), we excuse the behavior with an antiquated argument about heterosexual oppression and repressed homosexual need. We complain that park arrests for public indecency are not fair treatment by the police. Although the over-zealous harassment of the police is not enforced equally with non-gays, we nevertheless use their legalized bigotry to excuse our own failures, and criticize those who dare speak out against public sex as being old-fashioned moralists with their heads stuck in the sand. I wonder whose heads are really stuck in the sand.

We march, rally, demonstrate, lobby, and legislate to demand the equality we deserve; then, we turn around and perpetuate the stereotypes that keep us oppressed. This is not to suggest that we should behave as good little queers, rather it is about realizing that we're not children any longer; we are not liberation Lilliputians. We have reached that stage of middle-aged adulthood in our movement that demands a rational understanding of personal, social, and political responsibility.

It means that we must reject the stereotype of being sex-starved, promiscuous gays, by affording sex the respect it deserves in a mutually intimate relationship—and by acting as responsible adults while doing so. It means that we cannot continue to treat ourselves and each other as sexual objects to be fondled without permission (a common bar experience), or to be regarded as objects of impersonal sexual pleasure. It means that we dare not accept the porno-graffiti that so often permeates gay culture. It means that we must reject the mentality that leads us to believe that our only heroes dress like and insult women, and lip sync overly used, worn-out songs. And it means that we have to stop constantly competing for everything with a win-at-all costs mentality. It is unrealistic to hope that everyone might like everyone else; but we can at least try acceptance. We don't have to stab each other in the back, lie about the next guy, spread rumors about people we don't like, or negate people we really don't know simply because it is easier to identify ourselves as the oppressed than it is to define a nebulous, non-gay oppressor. It is time that we started thinking individually and about each other and our community as the strong, unified body that it can be.

We have, yet, a long road to travel and regardless of what some would have us believe, liberation is not just around the corner. Many of us will still die of AIDS-related illnesses. More of us will be bashed, discriminated against, and hated because we are gay. We will remain less than third class citizens until we get it together and shake the self-perpetuating defeatism that hangs around our neck like an albatross.

So let's grow up. Let's become the valuable, loving, sensitive, and caring people we really are. After all, it's a lot easier and intensely more rewarding to regard each other as intelligent and worthwhile individuals, than it is to continue seeing each other as immature, competing sex objects in a ruthless and frightening world.

Nobody likes to be criticized—not individuals and certainly not organizations. Few of us enjoy hearing negative comments about ourselves or the factions to which we belong. No one is especially enamored by suggestions that we should change our more unacceptable characteristics of personality, or the temperament of our organizations. But we do know that, ultimately, the only way to grow, the only way to become a better, more efficient, and more productive community is to listen to unfavorable criticism, learn from it, and work on changing those aspects of function that less than flatter our drive for liberation.

Thirteen
Monolithic Thought: Dare We Differ?

Have you ever felt that you were the only gay or lesbian who doesn't think the way you're supposed to think, or at least the way you were led to believe you were supposed to think? There seems to be an unwritten expectation within the G/L/B/T community that all of us are required to feel the same way about issues of both critical and inconsequential importance. The national gay media, as well many of our national organizations perpetuate such an attitude; often, so do we when talking with one another. But nothing could be further from the truth. In fact, the only things we gays share in common are sexual orientation, desire for equality, endurance of discrimination—and little else: not our politics, our religion, our values, or any one of a hundred other issues that reflect personal choice, rather than a single, monolithic gay perspective.

I don't know how many times I've heard another gay or lesbian whisper that he or she didn't agree with the prevailing consensus of community thought. Too often we drive newcomers away, simply because they don't tow the communal line. We fashion self-imposed, sociopolitical stereotyping, only to cry foul when those who oppress us do the same. We argue that there isn't such a thing as a typical gay person. We insist that all lesbians don't fit the same mold. We complain that heterosexuals see us as one dimensional, and yet we perpetuate the same by painting ourselves into a single-minded corner, making those who think differently feel as through they don't belong to the gay community.

How many gays or lesbians did you hear openly voicing support for the invasion of Iraq? Not many, and yet surely there had to have been some. But, according to the national gay media, the only correct gay response was to oppose Bush's imperialistic action. The fear of ostracism encourages silence.

How many times has it been implied that we should all embrace the politics of the Democratic or The Green Parties. It almost seems no one dare think otherwise; and according to mono-thought, there simply aren't any other viable politics—we are supposed to vote only for candidates who mimic the G/L/B/T political agenda completely; not people who represent our conscience.

It has become almost gay traitorous to be gay and Republican, or Roman Catholic, or evangelical, or pro-life, or any one of a score of other perceived-to-be less than desirable philosophies. Other than the occasional curiosity pieces about oddity gays, the national G/L/B/T media would have us believe that being homosexual and believing anything other than gay dogma is unacceptable.

How tragic for a community that claims to pride itself for its diversity.

As a community, we are supposed to fall in line—like lemmings on their way to the cliffs—daring not to speak out against unacceptable activities such as sex in the parks, but readily supporting the correct environmental issues, marching to the tune of the same drummer, endorsing nuclear disarmament (or any one of a dozen other perceived causes), and thinking that anything that smacks of patriotism is an unliberated sell out.

Well, it just ain't so.

The strength of our community stems from its blend of religion, philosophy, politics, attitudes, and values. Regardless of what our national media might have us believe, we don't all think alike, we don't all dress alike, we don't all listen to the same music, vote for the same politicians, or share similar values. And yet we perpetuate a single-minded mentality by assuming that we've developed a political subculture that somehow reflects everyone in the G/L//B/T community. Certainly, we have created a wonderfully diverse social culture that reflects our creativity, our spirit, and our history; and, thankfully, we haven't yet developed a political culture that speaks in concert with universal intellectual thought.

It is more constructive to share the cause of liberation with those who dare to think for themselves, rather than those who ape conformity. It is less pedestrian to be a part of a multi-dimensional blend, than to parrot single-minded accordance. It is more realistic to include differing ideas within the boundaries of the community, than to adopt a single tome that supposedly reflects everyone—and yet, no one. Imagine the prosaic uniformity of a community that mirrors the same politics, the same religion, the same everything—not very appealing, and certainly not an accurate representation of whom and what we really are.

When you get down to it, the only things we share in common are sexual orientation, the demand for equality, and an end to discrimination—and even those topics are hotly debated concerning how they should be approached. So be it—variety is, indeed, the spice of life. We constantly argue that we are no different from our heterosexual counterparts, so why not end the practice of simple-minded conformity.

Given a preference for open mindedness and individual thought, the next time you meet a gay Republican, welcome him into the fold. The next time you see a patriotic lesbian, embrace her with open arms. They may not reflect your exact views or your particulars of politics and philosophies that wax and wane, but they are, after all—us!

Fourteen
Civil Disobedience or Media Event?

In recent years, activists in the gay/lesbian community have embraced civil disobedience as a method for focusing media attention upon injustices directed against gays and lesbians. Throughout the last decade well-organized, highly publicized mass events have taken place in many cities around the United States and throughout Europe under the name of civil disobedience. But today's idea of civil disobedience has become a sanitized version of its original intention and functions more as ineffective media drama than it does a demonstration of moral conscience.

It used to be that civil disobedience meant breaking a specific law with which an individual had conscientious objection. Henry David Thoreau—the father of American civil disobedience—disobeyed civil laws on numerous occasions, first as a means of protest against the Mexican-American War, and later to enunciate his moral indignation with paying taxes that helped enforce the fugitive slave laws. He believed so strongly in his philosophies that he was willing to go to jail for his actions—and not just for a comfortable, pre-planned, few-hours visit, but for days and weeks of incarceration.

Scholars of civil disobedience argue that validating CD (civil disobedience) as a means of moral protest requires four characteristics basic to the act itself that distinguish it from clandestine criminal behavior. Those four are: (1) that the violation of law must be committed in public, (2) that the participant(s) accept the frame work of established authority and the general legitimacy of the system of civil law, (3) that non-violence separates civil disobedience from rebellion and revolution, and (4) that the specific law in question must be violated and not a law that is corollary to the one in question.

By accepting these historic characteristics as defining civil disobedience, it is easy to understand how Mohandas Gandhi's sitting in a whites-only section of a train in early 1900s South Africa was civil disobedience; or that suffragettes blocking the entrance to voting booths in 1920s America was civil disobedience; or that Rosa Parks committed civil disobedience by sitting in the white section of a bus in the 1950s; or that a group of black men, by taking their rightful places at a lunch counter in North Carolina, in 1960, committed civil disobedience; or that Joan Baez, by not paying telephone taxes during the Vietnam war because the taxes were used for weapons, was a civil disobedient; or that David Taylor kissing his lover in 1988 London, was a civil disobedient; or that Brian Wilson, losing his legs on a railroad track while blocking a munitions train, was a civil disobedient. Such effective acts of heroism and civil disobedience are not often the case anymore.

Today, the concept of civil disobedience has become confused with staging special events. The act of violating unjust laws has been replaced with slick, well organized, public relations—instant civil disobedience theater! Non-violent rallies, demonstrations, and parades are critical to the cause of the G/L/B/T liberation movement, but to argue that the arbitrary arrest of hundreds of demonstrators, protesting vague, corollary laws constitutes civil disobedience is absurd. Such ridiculous claims distort the definition of civil protest and demean those who's moral conscience and physical comfort has suffered personal hardship by disobeying particular laws and paying serious consequences.

Consider the mass demonstration and arrests on the steps of the United States Supreme Court in 1987 (in which I participated), at the Federal Drug Administration Building in

1988, at the numerous ACT-UP and Queer Nation CDs of the late 1980s and early 1990s, and more recently, the demonstrations at the IMF/World Bank Meetings. All have been billed as acts of civil disobedience, but few truly were. It is more than a matter of semantics, because few of the actions described above fit the definition of civil disobedience. Indeed, yes, the actions were committed in public. Yes, the participants accepted the legitimacy of the legal system, for if they had not, they would be rebelling against the established order, not simply disobeying it, and their actions would then be pathetically failed attempts at revolution. And yes, the actions were for the most part non-violent. But few of the actions violated the laws with which the violators had issue.

Certainly, it took courage for the participants of each action to commit to arrest—no one should question the sincerity or dedication of those involved. Most of the actions resulted in mass media coverage, both in the gay and in the mainstream press. Laws were broken, careers risked, and personal security jeopardized. But the reality is, as it is with most nationally organized arrest-events, the actions were simply—events! In many cases, the police helped plan the actions to reduce the incidence of potentially serious problems, misdemeanor charges were pre-arranged so no one had to remain in jail longer than necessary, the least common denominator of risk was negotiated. Punishment resulted in minimal fines, the media was invited to cover the events, and everyone was comfortable with the idea that the staged actions were little more than theatrical happenings.

For many participants in staged civil disobedience, involvement becomes little more than a three-ring circus that promises a day away from school or the job. Since research reveals that the majority of participants in recent G/L/B/T civil disobedience events are students or self-employed, one can honestly wonder just who is risking what? Of course, the purpose of contemporary civil disobedience is not as much to violate unjust laws, as it is to focus attention upon the "protest of the day," with as little risk as possible. Organizers of the 1987 CD event that shut down the U.S. Supreme Court (for the first time in its history) admitted that had legal charges not been arranged in advance and had participants not been guaranteed only a bothersome few hours in detainment (not even jail), few persons would have participated in the civil disobedience. The operative phrase in this confusing CD mess is, television exposure—1990s in-your-living room, orchestrated drama.

If the G/L/B/T community wants civil disobedience, then do it right: organize a public kiss-in in a state that still criminalizes same-sex intimacy. Arrange for mass confessions to acts of sodomy in places where laws continue to prohibit gay relationships (although curiously enough, not heterosexual sodomy). Stage the public marriage of hundreds of gay couples in a locale where being gay or lesbian is still against the law. And don't involve the cops with beforehand, pre-arranged misdemeanor charges and pay-by-mail fines.

Those would be true acts of civil disobedience—they directly violate the laws that keep us in bondage, and yet, in deference to the public relations minded, would still generate media coverage and focus attention upon the inequality of existing laws.

Of course such acts might also involve serious legal risk for the participants—a real problem for those who consider themselves street radicals, but who suckle from the breast they condemn, and live by the grace of the support of family and friends.

There is nothing wrong with a well-organized, cleverly focused, effectively reported demonstration, but let's call it what it is—a media event! After all, there have been brave men and women, of all liberation movements, who have risked their careers, their families, their security, and even their lives to disobey laws that were in conflict with a just society. I hardly think that the small fine I paid in the nation's capital in 1987 dares compare to the sacrifices of people like Rosa Parks, Maurice McCrackin, or Ralph Abernathy. More power to those in our community who take a risk for what they believe. If, however, the risk is but a staged risk for media exposure and not civil disobedience, then label it as such.

Fifteen
Where Have All the Heroes Gone?

Heroes: everybody needs them; some people have them. Countries have national heroes, children have storybook heroes, teenagers have sports, music, and movie heroes, adults have Walter Mitty heroes. But the G/L/B/T minority community suffers from a dearth of heroes, thereby confounding our attempt to rally a national force that could, theoretically, dwarf all other minority movements and eventually affect our goal of liberation.

The gay community can number its heroes on one hand, not because we don't have individuals who have assumed heroic proportion—certainly we do—but rather because our heroes are too few in number, much too far between, and mostly unknown to the majority of the gay community.

In an age when political conservatism is rampant and discrimination and violence are all too commonly directed against gay men and lesbians, heroes are in critical demand. However, there are too few legitimate candidates for reasons multidimensional in nature.

First, it is nearly impossible to transmit information about our community and thus our heroes when there are so few means of passing information from one gay person to another. The usual sociological and educational methods of cultural transmission are thwarted because our community has no

legitimate methods for educating younger gays and lesbians: not
through the schools, not through the family, not through the
church, and certainly not through societal role modeling. Those
avenues of information have been conveniently denied the gay
community. Generally, our way of learning about ourselves and
our history is through rumor, gossip, supposition, and the
occasional educational forum sponsored by a G/L/B/T
organization.

Second, too few gays and lesbians are willing to come out of
the closet and take the risks necessary to heroic accomplishment.
The fear of discrimination, social rejection, familial ostracism,
and economic devastation are too great.

Third, our leaders for the most part are administrators and
guardians of organizational policy, rather than visionaries with
an agenda for serious social change. The community needs
people who can administrate, but at this time in our history, we
are acutely more in need of heroes instead of civil servants.

Fourth, a national liberation movement really does not exist.
There are national organizations that accomplish important
goals, but like the leaders who administrate rather than lead,
they are for the most part lobbying organizations, information
clearing houses, and referral agencies.

Fifth, heroes are created by accident, by accomplishing
something out of the ordinary in the face of insurmountable
odds. They are not created by design in boardrooms by the vote
of committee.

And sixth, we gays fear accepting someone as a hero because
we fear entrusting one person with authority and moral
direction—perhaps because we cling to the antiquated theory of
ideological consensus (a noble, but unrealistic goal), or maybe
because we become jealous of the accomplishments of others who
distinguish themselves beyond what we, as individuals, dare.

Although we value the leadership of specific individuals on a
local (and sometimes national) level, we hesitate to consider
them heroes; thus, leaving us with a list of national possibilities
that reflect the best and the worst of our community. Consider
the candidates for gay/lesbian heroes:

Assassinated San Francisco Supervisor Harvey Milk[14] is,
indeed, a hero in the truest sense of the word. He was one of the

few gays who demonstrated that rare combination of ability, courage, bravery, and intelligence. He gave his life for what he believed—and he did so at a time in our history when it was not fashionable to come out and seek public office! Unfortunately, his heroics have been forgotten with time, and his name is little more than a whisper from the past for young gays and lesbians.

Marine Sergeant Leonard Matlovitch is another true hero. Sgt. Matlovitch fought the military and was ingloriously discharged from the Marines; then he battled for equal rights in court, and carried his struggle to the front lines of the gay movement—even to his death. And like Harvey Milk, he has become little more than a footnote in history.

Representative Gary Studds of Massachusetts is not a hero— a needed voice in legislative politics, undoubtedly, but not a hero. It is hardly heroic to admit one's homosexuality only after being caught with your hand in the cookie jar—or in his case down the pants of a House page.

Georgian Michael Hardwick of the 1986-87 Sodomy Case fame is a wannabe hero; certainly a celebrity, but a reluctant hero at best. Hardwick had the courage to battle his case all the way to the U.S. Supreme Court, but his ability to translate that courage into bravery and ability and to continue the fight long after the spotlight had faded has not been sustained.

Congressman Barney Frank is a hero-in-waiting: a man who declared his homosexuality without prodding, but tarnished his heroic status by admitting to keeping a male prostitute and drug user in an attempt to reform the young man. Come on Barney, let's be real—those are hardly heroic qualities. A little honesty never hurt a hero!

After that, there isn't much. There are names that come up again and again in the annals of gay and lesbian history: Kameny[15], Hay[16], Toklas[17], and Parker[18], and more, but most gays and lesbians are unaware of who these people are, and what their accomplishments involved.

Many dedicated activists are effective on local levels, but unfortunately, most of them go unnoticed by the community, ignored by the press, and are relegated to obscurity. They risk personal security to further the cause of liberation, but go unheeded and unnoticed. The problem is that few people know about them, and until their exploits become known, they aren't heroes—after all, heroes are larger than life; people know about them and their accomplishments and are inspired by their heroic deeds.

A sad corollary to identifying our heroes is that if you go into a typical gay bar on any given weekend night, and ask random patrons who some of the heroes of the gay community are, you'll most likely get responses like the cast from "Queer Eye for the Straight Guy," Madonna, Ellen DeGeneres, the cast of the Show Time series "Queer as Folk," male strippers, local drag queens, and national movie and recording stars (whether they are gay or not). Certainly what these people do is entertaining, perhaps even culturally significant, and obviously somewhat courageous. But to label them heroes commits serious injustice to those who have truly attained heroic accomplishment.

Gay and lesbian heroes cannot be invented. We cannot create a mythology of super stars. Most aspects of heroism are beyond our control—like establishing the necessary conditions for heroism, or creating heroic circumstances—but we can do more than we have.

First, we need to recognize individuals who have put personal security on the line in order to advance the cause of gay/lesbian liberation. We need to do more than simply pat them on the back and then forget their accomplishments the following week.

Second, we need to motivate people into coming out and taking the risks that lead to heroism. It might be true that no one has the right to drag another person out of the closet, but the pathetic attitude that argues that coming out is a personal choice, indifferent to common goals, has to stop. We will never develop any heroes and will never achieve our goals as long as we continue to make excuses for hiding in the closet.

Third, we must repeatedly create situations that encourage heroism; that is, take our cause into the courts, into the legislatures, into the classroom, into our churches, and into the streets. Waiting for our oppressors to grant us liberation is a waste of time. It may serve the best little queer in the world mentality quite effectively, but if we really want to accomplish our goals we need to escape the middle-class status quo and ignite the community with social revolution.

Fourth, we must look for vision in our leaders. We can always find enough business majors to administrate and accountants to add numbers, but discovering leaders who possess the qualities of vision and community is something, altogether, different. We may not be able to create heroes out of leaders, but we can encourage the heroic to come forward and the meek to become heroic.

And fifth, we must recognize that there are people who are fighting—and winning—everyday for the cause of gay liberation. We must give them their due.

Heroes are usually unintended. They do not see themselves as heroes. They frequently fall into the role by way of circumstance or situation, like Matthew Sheppard. And yet, we have little choice other than to encourage. We can continue the way things are. We can wage battles locally—city after endless city—and never unify as a national power. We can reject a potential leader out of jealousy or fear. We can continue plodding along the path of the status quo, or we can rally around people who express the vision and the hope that we all cherish so dearly.

There are heroes out there just waiting to be found, it is up to us to find them and follow.

Sixteen
In the Schools

Schools are supposed to be places where young people go to learn, grow, socialize, and mature. They are also institutions of society that challenge our youth into an acceptance of people and situations different from themselves. Ideally, schools should encourage an intellectual understanding of the world of which our youth are a part. On every level—primary, secondary, or collegiate—schools should demand academic integrity from those who lead, such that the young people who pass through their halls come out more worldly and more cognizant of the multicultural society in which they live. In most cases, our educational system lives up to those standards; in too many cases, it does not.

Two situations of which I am aware represent both the positive and the negative sides of the educational coin. I am compelled as a gay man by chance, an activist by choice, and an educator by profession to share these two fundamentally different tales. I am an instructor at a large university, but I've taught all levels of school: elementary, secondary, and college. Most of the time I'm proud to be a teacher; sometimes I am not. This first example that addresses the American educational system is one of those times when I am not so proud.

Brian's Story

In March 2001, an eighteen-year-old high school senior committed suicide. Sadly, in today's society, teenage suicide isn't a shocking story anymore; it is an all too common act of finality committed by desperate children, lost in a world they do not understand. As would be the case with any teenage suicide, his death left a void for those who loved him and caused a seemingly unanswerable mystery for his family and friends.

Brian (names have been changed) had been a model student. His litany of success and accomplishments reads like a page out of *Who's Who in America*, and surely, if there is such a thing as the All-American boy, Brian would have been that person.

His grades reflected dedication to intellectual accomplishment. He had been selected as a National Merit Scholar and had been accepted to a prestigious university. He was an accomplished pianist and played in his high school's concert orchestra. He was the starting quarterback on the Fighting Tigers football team. He ran track during the spring and was a member of a community swim team during the winter.

Brian served as senior class vice-president and had been elected to his high school Student Assembly for three years. He was active in his church and worked during the summer at a fast food restaurant. He was popular with his peers, and although he didn't date a great deal, he was considered the perfect catch by any one of the several hundred young women at his school. On the surface he seemed to have everything to live for—and that is why his suicide was so confusing and mysterious.

Two weeks after Brain was buried, one of his teachers found a letter tucked inside one of his textbooks. After reading the note, she gave it to Brian's guidance counselor, who in turn gave it to his parents. With confusion and surprise, his family, and eventually his friends, as well as the entire community where he lived, discovered the reason behind Brian's self-inflicted death. His note was later made public by his parents with hopes that it might prevent another tragic experience like Brian's. It read:

> To Whoever Cares?
> I can't go on living any longer with the pain and confusion of a split personality. On the one hand I am me; on the other hand, I am someone disgusting and perverted.
> Last week I broke up a fight between three of my classmates. Two of them were beating the shit out of the third guy who had just moved to our school. When I asked what was going on, my two buddies said, "Don't you know, this creep is a fag?" I ignored the situation and walked away,

letting them do what they felt necessary.

At football practice, last fall, the offensive line dubbed the tackling dummies Bugger Butts, a reference they made clear was directed at the "fucked up queers of the world." Coach just laughed and actually told 'em to pound the shit out of the dummies because they liked getting it up the ass.

In history class, one day, Mr. Smith told us about how gay people were burned at the stake in New England during the1600s and 1700s, and how they were put in prison and institutions during the nineteenth century in our own state. He even told us about how gays were gassed with the Jews by the Nazi's during World War II. Then he said that even today gays and lesbians don't have any rights. After his lecture, everyone laughed (some guys in the back of the classroom even applauded). Mr. Smith laughed too.

In health class, Mr. Adams explained the abnormal development of gay people and said their lives were a perversion of human nature.

In church, Reverend McCarthy preached that AIDS was God's punishment against the evil and sin of homosexuality.

Last week, I heard Dad and one of his friends making fag jokes and laughing as hard as they could.

Well, I've thought a lot about this and I'll make it easy on all of you—I'll save you the trouble of laughing at me. I can't take the pain anymore, knowing that I'm sinful and perverted—I don't want to be a freak of nature. I really don't feel like I'm so bad, but it doesn't seem to matter how I feel. I can't help the way I am; I didn't ask to be this way, but I am gay—a fag as my dad would say. I am one of the dirty queers everyone keeps telling jokes about.

I'm sorry if you don't understand. It's just that I can't deal with hurting everyone so much. I know my mom would be crushed. My dad would end up hating me. And who knows how everyone else would think.

Goodbye and don't cry.

Brian

As an educator, I am ashamed. As a gay man, I am infuriated. As a human, I weep. I am ashamed because as an educator, I know that our schools are bastions of heterosexist propaganda. They are rife with verbal harassment, physical violence, discrimination, prejudice, and bias—much of it directed against gays and lesbians. Research has demonstrated that our schools are one of the leading contributors to suicides among gay boys and lesbian girls. There is just too much hatred within the schools for gays and lesbians to react much differently. I am aware that in many larger city school districts, a number of policies have changed in favor of toleration and openness, but unfortunately, that does not apply to the vast majority of American schools in small town and rural America.

As educators, as friends we must ask ourselves whether or not this is the legacy we want to leave our children. A boy with a promising future is dead, and he is only one of many who will choose the ultimate exercise in futility as the answer to the pain, suffering, embarrassment, and discrimination caused by heterosexist bias.

The purpose of the educational system should be to provide for the development of intellectual, emotional, psychological, and physical student self-actualization. This philosophy should apply equally to all students within the public school community, regardless of age, gender, race, religion, ethnicity, physical challenge, or sexual orientation. Unfortunately, it does not. Our schools enact equality on an arbitrary and local basis. An unfulfilled promise of the American public educational community pertains to the lack of honesty and equality of opportunity as experienced by gay and lesbian students. Inherently defined as one of the paramount responsibilities of the school is the promise to provide equal educational opportunity for all students, with teachers functioning as the agents for learning, information, and change. Schools must develop methods of instruction and policy that insure that all students benefit from the educational experience—not just the chosen few of the controlling popular majority.

It is the responsibility of the educational community to assist and guide gay and lesbian students into becoming the kinds of adults of whom both they and society can be proud. Gay and lesbian adolescents are equally entitled to their rights as members of the community in which they live, and of the schools they attend. Gay and lesbian students are similar to their heterosexual friends, and yet they are different, but that difference need not brand them as social lepers in a world of heterosexist bias. They are, after all, our friends, our relatives, and our children—and we are slowly, methodically, and surely killing them.

When we look to place blame, we need search no further than inwardly, where we seem to manifest uncontrolled hate and fear. Let us hope, indeed, let us make certain that Brian did not die in vain, but brought a renewed sense of purpose and understanding to us all concerning the feelings and needs of gay and lesbian youth everywhere. Let's learn from Brian's death and insist upon change. Otherwise, our future generations will either mature into people similar to us, or will learn to look beyond our narrow definitions of humanity and stake claim on a world free of hatred, prejudice, and discrimination.

Letter from Cindy

A second experience that, in too few cases, typifies the American educational system concerns a letter I received from a young woman in one of my classes. Her experience makes me proud to be an educator. I'd like to share Cindy's letter (again, names have been changed) because I think it is applicable to all school settings; and besides, too often, we gays and lesbians get the idea that everyone in the non-gay world is against us. That isn't so, for many intelligent people will listen, learn, and change opinions. Cindy's letter goes like this:

I'm not really sure why I'm writing this, or what I want to say, but it is important to me that you know what I think about homosexuality.

When you came out to our class—that time after you got the hate letter from those jerk students—I told myself that I knew you were. I think I had known since the time you talked about the gay characters in that play we were studying and I made that dumb statement about queers being disgusting (by the way, my dad still doesn't think Edward Albee should be taught in college!).

After saying what I did, and then later, after you told the class that you were gay, I felt bad. I knew my comment made you think that I thought homosexuality was horrible. That isn't the case, at least not any more.

I accept and admire that you have accepted your sexuality. I also admire the fact that you were comfortable enough with us to tell about yourself (although most of us had guessed it already). It took a lot of guts to come out and tell your whole class. You had no idea how we would react or what we might say, but you had enough faith in our maturity (and pride in yourself) to disclose that information.

You are the best teacher I have ever had; you are also one of the coolest people I have ever met. The fact that you are gay has no bearing on my feelings for you as a person or as a teacher. I don't feel that a thing like sexual preference should change an established relationship whether it is a professional one or a personal one.

This whole experience has made me realize what you go through every day. You have to decide each time you meet someone if they are mature enough to handle your sexuality. That must be difficult not knowing if someone will hate you, or even punch you out.

I don't know why I felt like I had to write this note and tell you how I feel, but it is important to me to let you know what I said that time is not how I feel anymore.

I hope you understand. I have learned more in this class than just English. I told my dad about all this and he just grumbled something about how the university is teaching a gay agenda. But, even though I love my dad, he is wrong. I could never say that before, but now I can.

Thanks

Cindy

I don't share this letter because it is about me, because it could have been about any openly gay or lesbian teacher. I share it because it says a great deal about *us* and *them*.

Although I take exception to Cindy's use of the phrase sexual preference, rather than sexual orientation, her letter exemplifies a young woman who obviously learned and matured a great deal in a short period of time. She says something important.

Early in my professional association with Cindy, she seemed to indicate, through one of her comments during a class discussion, that she thought homosexuality was disgusting. That isn't terribly unusual coming from a non-gay who has been reared on heterosexism and homophobia—a lack of education contributes to all forms of prejudice, discrimination, and misunderstanding. But during Cindy's first year in college, she matured and grew.

I don't know for certain, but I would guess that I am Cindy's first close association with someone who is openly gay. Contrary to what many people believe about heterosexuals, Cindy didn't use our association to reinforce the stereotypes with which she had been raised.

She learned to see beyond sexuality and accept a teacher she respects and admires. I couldn't hope for more. Cindy embodies the process of experience, learning, and change, which the best type of education encourages.

To gay and lesbian teachers, Cindy's letter should serve as education. In her short note, she identifies at least three cogent points that can help each of us learn to feel better about ourselves and learn to celebrate the identify we so often hide.

First, regardless of what we sometimes want to think about the non-gay world, there are many people out there who are supportive, who admire what we contribute to society, and who respect us for the courage we demonstrate by living openly.

Second, Cindy's letter reminds us of how important it is to be honest about our lives. The controversy that surrounds coming out can be argued with legitimate passion for remaining closeted, but case in point—Cindy's letter shows all too well how being open and honest cannot only function as the magic elixir for our own sanity and happiness, but can serve as a conduit through which understanding and education can occur between gays and non-gays.

Third, Cindy's letter should make us realize how critical it is to celebrate who we are. It is not enough to reluctantly accept our sexual orientation—there really isn't anything we can do to change it anyway—however, being proud, being strong, and being happy with ourselves is paramount to the realization of individual success, hope, and the promise of what can be.

Too often, those of us who fancy ourselves gay activists become hardened to the sensitivities of cross-orientation friendships. We tend to think in an us-vs.-them mentality, a battle cry of bitterness and hostility. Sometimes we forget that we have more support than we want to recognize, and when we forget, we become frustrated with the slow progress of liberation.

It is invigorating to receive a message like Cindy's. Such messages remind us that our struggle is worthwhile. Such messages make real the fact of being one in the family of human kind, and from such messages we derive hope and encouragement for the long struggle ahead.

Give Cindy's letter some thought; let her message afford you the opportunity to celebrate who you are. Cindy didn't reinforce disgust and prejudice when she discovered her teacher was gay. She didn't shy away in fear. She didn't let the stereotypes of a lifetime of misinformation contradict that which she had come to know.

Instead, she embraced change, welcomed the chance to experience something different, and accepted a fellow human, based solely upon respect. If that isn't encouraging, then I don't know what is.

To gay and lesbian teachers everywhere—be proud and be strong. Celebrate who you are and give yourself the opportunity to be open. And to Cindy, thanks; I needed your encouragement and honesty.

Seventeen
The New Radical Activism

In the past few years, younger gays and lesbians throughout the United States (and indeed throughout the world) have become infused with a new sense of purpose and political consciousness; a new spirit of social and political activism is sweeping the community.

In city after city, and in areas once unorganized and under-represented, new groups like Queer Nation, ACT-UP, and the Lesbian Avengers (to name but a few; so many pop up here and there by the week) have spawned to form the nucleus of what appears to be a renewed sense of radical politics and urgency. Most of the new groups are aggressive in nature, militant by agenda, and activist in orientation. The spirit of radical action that typified the early days of the gay/lesbian liberation movement has reemerged in the hearts and minds of thousands of younger men and women who have grown weary of what they regard as traditional go-slow politics.

Not surprisingly, the reaction from established gays and lesbians has been one of suspicion and disdain for the radicalism of these groups, the militancy of their agenda, and the irreverence of that which they regard as establishment power. Why, ask they, for whom the movement has become middle-aged like themselves, does the G/L/B/T community need confrontational new groups to represent our concerns? Why, wonder they, who have worked so long and hard for the current success, is there even a need for different groups to exist? Don't these new groups duplicate efforts? The answers to such questions, though multidimensional in nature, replicate life itself.

Similar to the middle years of an adult's life, existing gay G/L/B/T political organizations (in some cases) have grown complacent with age. Their once keen sense of idealism has been blunted with political expediency. The activism that once characterized a demand for change has been replaced with plodding, monolithic practicality; and now, rather than welcoming the call for political revival, the better entrenched in the community prefer to bask in success and maintain the status quo. And, similar to the quest for midlife security, some middle-aged G/L/B/T organizations would rather expend energy in the areas of economic solvency, organizational status, and political prestige (elements that although managerial, are still critical to liberation).

The extreme stages of human life–youth and old age–have historically contributed more to the cause of human achievement than has middle age. More famous scripts of literature, more tantalizing scores of music, and more beautiful pieces of art have been produced by either the young or the old. More inventions, discoveries, and technological breakthroughs have been advanced by youth and old age. More cures for diseases, more political ideologies, and more spiritual ennui have been spirited by those under thirty-five and beyond the age of sixty. It is unfortunate, but true, that in the vast, nebulous span of life called middle age, there have been fewer major contributions that have aided the cause of social evolution.

Much the same can be said about the evolution of organizations. When an organization first begins, it is replete with energy, idealism, a sense of urgency, and a strong commitment to the cause; it is propelled by individuals whose activism matches the philosophy. As organizations age, however, and as they grow into a self-sustaining organism, the idealism wanes. Not because of dampened commitment on the part of its members; but rather because perseverance becomes more important than impatience, maintenance more appealing than change, pragmatism more desirable than idealism, expediency more necessary than urgency, and comfort more tenable than inconvenience. In short, the status quo becomes more enviable than radical activism: a political microcosm of every day life!

This is not to suggest that middle-aged gay political organizations do not serve the community well. Quite the contrary. In most cases they have established important relationships with the powers that be, they are capable of raising necessary money from sources unavailable to the more radical groups, and they are able to wield power and prestige in a way that fledgling organizations can only envy.

But at the same time, middle-aged organizations must either change to reflect the needs and concerns of the contemporary world or step aside to permit the more idealistic members an opportunity to initiate metamorphosis. That's the way it is with life, and that is the way it must be with organizations.

Suffice to say, the idea of change should not be troublesome for the middle-aged, for youth and idealism are the ingredients that ignite evolution; whereas, age and wisdom are the elements that temper caprice. Although the experience is painful, organizations must maintain their sense of activism—not only for the sake of the community, but for their own survival as well. A changing community has to be represented by organizations equal to the challenge of social evolution. They must either cooperate in an effort to foster change or become extinct like the dinosaurs that time (and natural catastrophe) erased.

But just as long-existing organizations must make room for youth and idealism, the newer and more radical groups must appreciate the struggles, the successes, and the tribulations experienced by people who began fighting long before being out was socially acceptable. Being middle-aged does not have to be equated with complacency. Experience need not be disregarded. Wisdom should never be ignored.

Realistically, no single organization can expect to meet the concerns of an entire community. No single organization can hope to represent all of the people, all of the time. If such a group were to exist—if one organization could establish itself as the foremost among peers, whether it is radical in nature, or

methodical by purpose—then it must readjust organizational
mentality and redirect energy toward unified activism.

Certainly there is room in the G/L/B/T community for
multiple political organizations. Our differences should be used
to our benefit, not at our expense. We can function, together even
when separated by political philosophy. Since we claim to be
everywhere and refreshingly diverse, we must, also, capitalize on
our political and philosophical rainbow blend.

But let us not forget that only through unity and strength
can we succeed; for without the bond that links us to the
common cause for which we have so long struggled, we will
surely be defeated. Diversity is not competition and change is not
insurgency; neither, then, should the young be regarded as a
threat, nor the established with suspicion. We must go forward,
driven neither by the fears of middle age nor by the inexperience
of youth, but rather empowered by the concept of community
that has long exemplified our struggle.

An era of renewed activism has emerged. A new spirit is
loose in our community. A new urgency has been spawned—an
urgency from which we dare not turn. I hope we will rise to the
call, blend the wisdom of age with the energy of youth, and heed
the winds of change.

Eighteen
Let's Hear It for Religion!

Recently, I met a young man who is affable, intelligent, humane, and deeply spiritual. Unfortunately, for him, he is also gay. My radar went off immediately upon meeting him and was later confirmed as being accurate by my friend who acknowledged his buddy's gay orientation. The two men work together, have begun socializing, and entertain a running discussion about religion, God, the Bible, and this young man's church. I have become privy to their conversations by way of discussion with my friend, who spills the proverbial beans without betraying the exact content of their conversations. What he shares with me is a tragedy of individual proportion. This friendly, life-seeking young man remains ensconced deep in the closet, fearful that should he venture out he will be condemned by his church, rejected by his friends, and disowned by his family. His religion has convinced him that he is a sinner, that homosexuality is vile, and that God will punish him with eternal damnation should he ever act on his sexual inclinations. Wow, what a pathetic way to regard God: a petty, self-serving deity that creates then condemns one of its own creations. And all along I thought God was supposed to be omniscient and loving.

This young man's life has become a living hell. He has expressed an understanding of whom and what he truly is. He has minimally delved into the world of gay sexual behavior. He

admits that he is attracted to men, not to women. And he is
learning the language and mannerisms that reflect the more
stereotypical side of homosexuality (behavior not uncommon
when a man first discovers his gay identity). But he can't shake
the religious indoctrination that condemns gays—himself—to a
life of despair and an eternity of damnation. His church has done
quite a job.

Having been raised in a religious family, with the fear of God
deeply entrenched in my young psyche, I understand the pain
this young man is going through. It took me years to come to an
understanding of God and to develop a personal spirituality. It is
difficult to separate from the teachings and scriptural passages
that are randomly selected from the Bible and hurled from the
pulpit like lightening bolts from Heaven.

How convenient for those who prefer pontificating over
understanding and who also stand in judgment of those born
with a minority sexual orientation. How opportune to pick and
choose the scriptures that supposedly condemn homosexuality,
while ignoring the central meaning of Biblical stories such as
Sodom and Gomorrah or David and Jonathan. How expedient to
forget that the Savior of the Christian World—Jesus Christ—
never once spoke about or even obliquely referred to the issue of
homosexuality. How fitting to overlook that God—who possesses
neither male nor female, but is the supremacy of both genders—
created us in Its image. Doesn't that apply to gays and lesbians
as well?

Certainly, there are Christian denominations that take a
theologically liberated view of homosexuality. The Unitarian-
Universalist Church (though not strictly Christian, but more
akin to Reformed Judaism), the United Church of Christ, the
Metropolitan Community Church, the more enlightened faction
of the Episcopal Church, and the Society of Friends welcome
gays and lesbians and allow full participation in church
ceremony, ritual, and sacraments. Protestant denominations like
the Lutheran Synod, the Presbyterian Church, and the United
Methodist Church, as well as the Greek Orthodox Church and
the Roman Catholic Church welcome gay parishioners, but
continue to insist that we remain celibate—eunuchs with
genitals—and deny some sacraments to gays and lesbians.

At the same time, there are those such as the Southern Baptist Convention, the Church of Jesus Christ of Latter-day Saints (the Mormon Church), and many other sects of fundamentalists and evangelicals whose history of condemnation is about as far removed from the teachings of Jesus Christ as one can get, and whose official stance still condemns us as sinners destined to burn in Hell for eternity. Other world religions take a more enlightened view, with the notable exception of Islam and Orthodox Judaism. Hinduism, Buddhism, and the vast majority of the world's tribal and Native American religions regard homosexuality as commonplace, normal, and acceptable.

For thousands of years gays have been tormented, condemned, vilified, and abused by the Christian religion among others—certainly Christianity does not have a market on denunciation. We were tortured during the Spanish Inquisition. We were burned at the stake by colonial Puritans. We were gassed by Hitler's Nazis. We were murdered in Stalinist Russia. We were slaughtered by Pol Pot in Cambodia. And still today, we are mugged, beaten, verbally abused, and denied our civil liberties in a nation that prides itself on being "One Nation Under God" and on bestowing equal rights and opportunity to all. All the while religion either directly participated in the atrocities perpetuated against gays and lesbians or idly stood by with its ostrich head buried in the sand. Such behavior makes me wonder who really will be called to judgment!

I have no problem with religious people who practice their faith in an honest, loving, and Christ-like way. My family and most of my friends are among that type. Those with whom I have problems are the self-righteous who take it upon themselves to interpret the Word of God as though they were privy to God's intentions, who selectively pick and choose scripture for the purpose of justifying their sanctimonious beliefs, who pass judgment on anyone with whom they disagree, and who deny the sacraments of the church to individuals whose sexual orientation is not hetero.

The road to Hell is, indeed, paved with supposedly good intentions. The wicked are truly among us, and evil is a powerful aphrodisiac. But gays and lesbians are not, by nature, traveling the road to Hell. We are neither wicked nor evil. We are no more sinful than any other person of Christian ideology, and our sins are not caused by being homosexual—as some Christians would have us believe—but are the same kinds of sins committed by everyone else on a daily basis. Indeed, the true blasphemy rests with those who would speak for God, not through God.

It is a black mark against any church that denies some of its parishioners equal participation and equal standing. It is a sin against God to condemn and judge in Its name. It is an embarrassment to religion that gays and lesbians have had to turn to spiritual organizations outside most of the Christian denominations simply to participate in the worship of God. God's church has been kidnapped. Its words have been twisted. Its will is not being done. In the name of God, some Christians have perverted God's meaning and reshaped it into the church of, for, and by man. The possibility of a beautiful, simple belief in the teachings of Jesus Christ has been reinvented as hateful nonsense by those who refuse to accept all people as children of God.

How curious to consider that those who have perverted God's will spend more time condemning than they do praising. Obviously, they rush to their respective churches on Sunday morning to participate in praise of the Lord, but leave that same church after the last hymn has been sung to re-enter their world of hypocrisy—quick to wag fingers at those with whom they disagree. Many pompous Christians are also the most condemning, the most hate filled, and the most ignorant. Too many contemporary Christians have become so fearful that they conveniently label whatever they do not comprehend as sinful and ungodly. But therein rests the history of that kind of believer. These are the same people whose ancestors defended slavery in the name of the Bible and of God. These are the same people whose forbears relegated women to second-class citizenship in the name of the Bible and of God. These are the same people who forced Native Americans out of their spirituality. These are the same people who congregated at Matthew Sheppard's funeral—after he was brutally raped and murdered by God-fearing heterosexual men—because he was gay. These are the same people who reflect Jesus Christ in their smiles, but live with hatred and fear in their hearts.

Christianity is not the problem. God is not the quandary. Many good and admirable people practice their Christian faith in an open and loving manner. The church has conducted thousands of humanitarian missions. Religion has led many millions from a life of emptiness to self-fulfillment and spiritual revelation. To those who would condemn Christian denominations as a whole, I advise restraint—it is not faith that is at fault, but the institution created by man in the name of God. It is not we who were created in the image of God who are at fault, but the God who has been created in our image.

To those in the church who would rather condemn than to accept, who would rather pontificate than communicate, and who would rather judge than be judged, I say be done with you and take your leave from the temple Christ built. The G/L/B/T Community is inclined to think that your place is not at the table of the Lord, nor even in Heaven, that your damnation of others has sealed your fate.

The young man, of whom I wrote earlier, has a long, lonely road to travel—that is if he chooses to walk his path alone. There are millions of God-loving Christians who would be willing to walk with him and help carry his cross until he reaches Earthly peace and understanding. But his cross is not one of sin and punishment enacted by a vengeful God; it is a cross foisted upon his shoulders by people who assume they speak for God.

For those of you who are like this young man, I ask you to take a moment, today, tonight, or whenever you choose, and talk with God. In this way, you may find peace and understanding and come to know God's love. I think that God will answer and the words might be: I created you as you are, from the image of my omniscient being. You are not a sinner because of who you are; you are my child as much as anyone else is my child. If you truly believe in Me, if you truly believe that I created you...then why do you labor? Why do you toil over the condemnation of humankind? If you do not believe in My love and My Word, then why come to Me with your pain and sorrow? If you accept vilification, then surely you reject me as the Creator of this universe. Would you rather believe in a god created in the image of man, or in the Truth that I am? If I were to create you and then condemn you for what I have created, then I am flawed and not the God you seek. But I am not flawed, for I am God; therefore, live in peace and know always that I love you.

Nineteen
Amos and Andy, Meet Will and Jack

When I remember back to the early days of television I remember how horribly gays and lesbians were depicted—if depicted at all! We weren't given any significant roles save the occasional sissified butler, the serial killer dyke, the strange bachelor who lived up the lane (and whom children were supposed to avoid), or the frumpy uncle who came to visit only on holidays. From the 1950s through the early 1990s openly gay and lesbian roles on TV were as scarce as straight men at a White Party at Key West. Of course, insightful viewers were able to pick out the queers, even though no characters were mentioned as being homosexual; we were stereotyped in terms of how gays and lesbians were regarded during that era. When we weren't being cast as crazed, depressed, lunatics, we were presented as pitiful, sad, lonely, and deranged people.

For the most part, television capitalized on the ignorance that surrounded homosexuality during the early and mid years of the idiot box's popularity. The highly rated medical drama, "Marcus Welby, M.D." aired two episodes about gay men: in one episode Dr. Welby counseled a distraught young husband that with proper psychiatric care the man could change his homosexual orientation; in another, a gay science teacher was portrayed as a child molester and pedophile. Other programs depicted gays and lesbians as crazed killers ("Police Woman"), eunuchs ("Love, Sidney"), insulting pretenders (Jack on "Three's Company"), or fastidious neurotics (Uncle Arthur on "Bewitched").

Of course there were the few exceptions to the rule: "N.Y.P.D." in 1967 was the first serious program to portray gays in a sympathetic manner and the first TV program to utter the word homosexual in a dramatic context. In 1977 "Soap" debuted Jodi Dallas (played by Billy Crystal), a relatively normal and sane young man as compared to the heterosexual characters on the show. There were also a handful of made-for-TV movies that tackled the issues of homosexuality with courage and honesty: *That Certain Summer* (1972), *A Question of Love* (1978), *Consenting Adult* (1985), and *An Early Frost* (1985). As television matured, it offered additional television movies such as *What Ever Happened to Billy?*, and *Doing Time on Maple Drive*. Nevertheless, for the most part, television feared the wrath and retribution of conservative organizations bent on preserving "solid, American values" and stayed as far away from gay reality as possible.

Little by little things began to change as gays and lesbians became more open and more accepted by middle-class America. From the mid-1980s and into the 2000s gay and lesbian characters began to appear more openly on television programs such as "NYPD Blue," "The Simpsons," "Law and Order," "Desperate Housewives," "The OC," "Survivor," and of course, "Ellen." Cable programming contributed the likes of "The L Word," "Queer as Folk," and "Queer Eye for the Straight Guy," increasing our exposure and presenting us in a more positive light. More recently, cable and satellite executives latched on to the growing popularity of gay programming and offered networks directed specifically at the gay and lesbian audience.

Historically, it had been regarded as the kiss of death for a television network to float a gay-themed program, a director to direct one, or an actor (particularly a male) to portray a gay character. It wasn't that TV-land was unaware of gays and lesbians—quite the contrary, television was rife with gay and lesbian writers, directors, producers, actors, and scores of ancillary employees—rather it was that gay didn't sell. Gay-themed television didn't attract significant sponsors, mainly due to the threat of boycotts by religious moralists and political right-wing organizations. Besides, the viewing pubic wasn't ready for what they might behold. Women didn't want to fantasize about the current leading hunk kissing another man, and men didn't dare admit that the macho he-man they admired had played a sissified queer. It just didn't make for good revenue, and revenue means success...success means money...and money means you have to have straight characters kissing other straight characters, the leading man getting the woman (or hunting down the latest rapscallion), and acceptable themes about love, crime, war, aliens from outer space, or any one of a thousand other plots that reflected the real world as the majority of heterosexuals would like to believe.

But all was not to be forever lost! As gays and lesbians began to organize and gain a modicum of political clout, as more and more sisters, brothers, children, aunts, and uncles came out of the closet, Middle America discovered that we were indeed everywhere and that our stories sometimes made for entertaining drama and humor similar to that portrayed in heterosexual-themed programs. Still, in most cases, gays and lesbians continued to play the roles of depressed, lonely, and unsavory characters that ended up committing suicide or miraculously changing their sexual orientation and being whisked away—forever in love—with a member of the opposite sex.

Then, out of the realization that gay programming could be profitable (gay money spends as well as straight money, and there are a heck of a lot of gay and lesbian viewers) networks discovered that gay just might sell, and suddenly there appeared a plethora of supporting gay characters on sit-coms and on a handful of dramatic programs (most of the shows being short lived, however). Most notably since the turn of the millennium, the Warner Brothers Television Network (WB) and Fox have been adding gay and/or lesbian characters to their store of teen-angst programs, as well as on cop, lawyer, and medical shows.

It seems that the younger generation has become more comfortable with dealing with the gay identity than had the baby boom generation! Still, I have serious reservations about the veracity of gay life, as depicted by gay characters, on most network television, and I have serious reservations about what motives are actually behind the networks that run gay-themed programs. It certainly isn't motivated by a sense of humanity, it obviously isn't generated out of a desire to promote equality, and it surely isn't provoked by a need to allow for the creative and artistic representation of gay life. Rather it is because right now, at this time in American history, gay is popular.

Consider the fashions that originate in the gay community and pass into the straight (most straight boys don't want to deal with that reality). Think about the concept of meterosexuality that seems to have taken metropolitan areas by storm. Consider the accoutrements of fashion such as earrings, nipple rings, and jewelry that never would have been worn by heterosexual men, until they became the latest popular fad. There is even, now, a phenomenon of straight teenagers coming out as gay because it's the cool thing to do and draws immediate attention (of course that "cool" orientation changes quickly once the fad has worn off because people begin to assume the guise is true or a desirable member of the opposite sex comes along).

It is true that gay is currently popular and more openly accepted in many parts of the country (in the bigger cities, but not in small town or rural America); therefore, the networks—eager to draw an audience for the products that sponsor their programs—hop on the queer bandwagon and pander to the masses, but what they pander isn't gay reality!

Gay reality is realizing that every day, every time you meet someone new, you have to come out of the closet all over again. Being gay isn't sitting in a restaurant with Will, Grace, and Jack acting like stereotypical goofballs for the patrons who surround them.

Gay reality is wondering when your rights to a job or housing or safety will be compromised by the bigot down the street, your landlord, or a group of thugs looking for a queer head to bash. It isn't stealing a secret boy-to-boy kiss on "The OC."

Gay reality is knowing that at any time, for any concocted reason, the controlling majority can take away what few rights we have. It isn't getting caught up in some harebrained scheme by the latest dopey gay character in a trail of fag funny fops.

Gay reality is being scared to death to come out to your parents, your siblings, and your friends for fear of losing their love and friendship. It isn't giggling like silly buffoons on a twenty-three minute sit-com.

Gay reality is understanding that many religions consider you a sinner and pound your self-esteem into the ground Sunday after never ending Sunday. It isn't having your local clergyman making a sudden change of heart about you being queer on "Seventh Heaven."

Gay reality is knowing that you can be beaten, your property compromised, your integrity called into question, and your sense of self-worth pummeled into obscurity. It isn't laughing away at the stereotypes on "Queer Eye for the Straight Guy."

Gay reality is growing old, having the typical aches and pains common to all people, losing your hair, adding a few inches to your waistline, and having to scrape by on social security. It isn't being forever young in a make-believe world of teenage beauty.

Certainly, there is something to be said about exposure, even if it's misleading and inadequate. At least gays and lesbians are being seen in a light better than that of a mass murderer, a psychopathic maniac, a child molester, or a depressed, lonely, pitiful boob. But it's not enough! Despite the offerings of The WB, Fox, the traditional big three (CBS, ABC, and NBC), or isolated cable networks, gays and lesbians continue to remain little more than mindless entertainment, produced by money-motivated studios, and watched by an unknowing, ignorant audience.

The quintessential gay-themed program of the past several years has been the NBC hit, *Will and Grace*. The show has been typically among the top rated sit-coms on TV. Audiences tune in week after week to see what hapless scheme Will or Jack get themselves into.

We chuckle, we giggle, and we laugh at their silly antics. We love the gay banter that Will and Jack bubble back and forth at one another. We empathize when Jack makes a fool of himself at one of his performance shenanigans. But we recoil in horror when Will partners with a scripted permanent mate. It's just not right! Will isn't supposed to have a stable relationship—he's

Will, the successful, witty, charming attorney, not Will with genitalia.

The network was deluged with complaints when the writers partnered Will with an apparently permanent boyfriend. No one wanted to see Will as a functioning, homosexual human being. It was all right when he was dating, and breaking up week after week—we felt sorry for him: Poor guy just couldn't seem to meet the right person. But when he did, Katie bar the door! It forced us to think about...well...umm...two men in love! It made us wonder what they might be doing behind that closed bedroom door. It demanded that we accept Will as a person—not a stereotypical queer—but as a human being complete with the same needs, desires, and hopes that his heterosexual counterparts share.

And so, Will's boyfriend was written off the series. Now he's back to being the good old homo boy down the hall. He's intelligent. He's handsome. He's affable. He's everything in a man you'd like to take home to introduce to your parents—if you are a woman, not a queer. They might as well change the name of the show to Eunuch and Grace. After all, Middle America can laugh at a homosexual as long as it doesn't have to think of him as being sexual. The network neutered Will like we would our pet cat. Now we can watch him play around the house, entertain us, and make us laugh...but gosh darn, he better not have any thoughts about sex!

And so it goes. Gays and lesbians continue to be victimized by an industry that cares more about making money than it does creating reality. Only now, rather than being crazed, child-molesting, psychopathic, depressed killers...we're silly, glittering hood ornaments that help the majority of heterosexuals forget their problems and breathe a sigh of relief that at least they aren't queer. We have come part of the way to television liberation, but not all of the way. Until the day arrives when we are presented on television as normally functioning human beings, we still have a long road to travel.

Certainly, there will be those who disagree. There will be those who argue that something is better than nothing. There will be those who insist that gays on television provide role models for gay boys and lesbian girls. There will be those who claim that we've finally been accepted into the mainstream of American life.

Right! Just like Native Americans were depicted as homicidal, drunken, scalp-seekers during the heyday of TV westerns; not as the spiritual, loving people they really are. Just like television depicted Hispanics as overly emotional, '57 Chevy-loving white Latinos, rather than the intelligent, hard working citizens they are. Just like television depicted women, and blacks, and a dozen other minority people as normal, everyday Americans during the golden years of the idiot box.

Not so long ago, there were those who argued that black face minstrel shows and "Amos and Andy" weren't all that bad—at least African Americans were being recognized. And indeed they were—as silly side-kicks, dancing yes-men, loyal butlers, ghost-fearing sissies whose eyes grew larger than pie plates at the sight of a hobgoblin, and bubble-brained idiots whose sole purpose was to serve as the foil for the much more intelligent white character. Meanwhile, an entire generation of Americans bought into the stereotypes portrayed in those obscene productions that set back the cause of African American liberation another fifty years.

Such is the same for current gay and lesbian programming, so let's suck up our pride, pander to the stereotypes, and let out a big cheer for "Will and Grace!" After all, Amos and Andy have to have someone to hang around with.

Twenty
The Quilt

The AIDS Quilt has come and gone from communities around the country, ending up in Washington, DC every several years or so, to be displayed for thousands of mourners and the curious. The effort of those who have worked so hard on this living memorial to those who have died from the horror of AIDS has paid dividends ten times over as people of all ages, ethnic backgrounds, politics, and orientations crowd together to view the display. For the scores of friends, lovers, and relatives who come to honor those memorialized on the patchwork shrine, the Quilt symbolizes a rainbow blend of art and beauty that will forever commemorate their loved ones. The Quilt has been an emotional, personal, and communal success. What it stands for is good, but what it has become begs the original intention of its creators.

I've heard many people say that the Quilt has become a living memorial to those who have died of AIDS. I've heard others say that out of this terrible plague has arisen a beautiful testament to our humanity. And I've heard still others claim that the Quilt has bound our community together with a sense of purpose and commitment seldom experienced. It's hard to argue with sentiment like that. It's hard to examine what the Quilt has become without being blasphemous. It's awkward to raise questions when everyone has become engulfed in the hysteria of Quiltism. Questioning the reality of the Quilt is like telling dead baby jokes; in the gay community, it's tantamount to treason.

I can't help wondering if the Quilt really does represent the sentiments we hear so eloquently vocalized. I can't help wondering if the Quilt hasn't become more a symbol of our worst fears than a testament to our resolve. I can't help wondering why we've allowed such a moving memorial to become little more than a traveling road show. I can't help wondering why we've permitted the volunteerism that originally surrounded the Quilt to become just another excuse for hawking souvenirs. I can't help wondering why we've turned viewing the Quilt into a quasi-religious experience. I can't help wondering why we wait until our friends are dead to show them the love and respect they deserved while they lived.

It's enigmatic to our community that we so carefully avoid reference to the concept of a deity—except when blaming the bigoted ideas of man's religion on God—as we attach ritual and religious ceremony to the Quilt. The Quilt has become sacrosanct; it's regarded as a holy artifact, and a symbol that we dare not question.

On the one hand, we criticize the Christian denominations for condemning healthy, theological skepticism, yet blindly defend the Quilt as being beyond reproach. In fact, many of the same people who disdain the concept of God, approach the Quilt with a reverence normally reserved only for religion. We've turned the ceremony and ritual associated with the Quilt into a religious experience. Consider the somber, almost morbid, reading of names when the Quilt is unveiled at various locations, the synchronized and ritualized unfolding of the panels, the priestly white garb worn by volunteers, and the hushed tones and expressionless faces that view the display.

During one of my several visits to the Quilt, I almost expected to see someone from the National Quilt Organizing Committee come out swinging an incense burner, chanting a mantra, and sprinkling holy water over the panels. I can't believe that this is what Cleve Jones had originally intended. Certainly the Quilt is intended to memorialize, but it is also supposed to be a symbol of celebration for the lives of those who have departed. Generally, celebrations are not somber, other worldly, mystical experiences such as has become synonymous with the AIDS Quilt.

For thousands of years humankind has sought to make sense out of death—we attach symbol and significance to realities otherwise normal, in an attempt to comfort and explain—but with the Quilt, we seem to have invented a contemporary, secular ceremony that canonizes the dead. It is popular—and even socially acceptable—to criticize the primitive rituals that surround death as practiced by organized religion (when someone we love isn't involved), but we dare not question the same concepts now created by the Quilt.

And what about the garish selling of souvenirs? The National Names Project organizers have become little better than the right-wing televangelists that our community is so quick to criticize. On the one hand, we disdain hawking religious artifacts in the name of the Lord, while on the other hand we defend shameless Quilt hucksterism as a necessary fundraising evil. Doesn't that smack of the same rationale used by televangelists?

Obviously, in order to move the Quilt to various locations around the country, funds have to be raised, but, rather than seeking grants, organizing large-event fundraising, promoting donations, and charging admission to the display, the National Names Project Committee hawks books, buttons, banners, bumper stickers, posters, T-shirts, and anything else that might generate capital, then excuses it all as a necessity. I dread what might come next: small pieces of celebrity Quilt panels for sale? Hey, don't laugh—it could generate thousands of dollars, and haven't some church organizations been generating money for centuries by selling religious artifacts?

I also wonder why we so often wait until people are dead to demonstrate our feelings for them. The Quilt serves as a perfect example of our hypocrisy, but I guess that's just a part of human nature. Of course psychologists tell us that a great deal of after-death fixation can be attributed to guilt. What a curious thought!

Example: Like many in the gay community, I've known a number of people who have died of AIDS-related complications—one man in particular comes to mind. He had few friends and few defenders of his personality. He was a gossip and was always critical of those around him. In life, he was not well regarded. He was, in fact, petty, nasty, and spiteful. But, in death, he has become everyone's friend and a leader of his community—he's even had several Quilt panels made for him. He would probably wonder: why did they wait so long to speak kindly of me? I wonder why only in death has he become loved, why not in life?

Now, lest anyone misunderstand what I am saying, rest assured that I strongly support the Names Project Quilt—I just don't like what it has become. Cleve Jones's original idea of creating a monument to the lives of those who have died of AIDS-related complications remains a touching and beautiful memorial. The Quilt has brought together many people who otherwise would not have confronted their own mortality. It has touched the hearts of many callous souls; after all, a person cannot see the Quilt and not be changed. But I hope that change means dedicating time, energy, and resources to eradicating this disease.

I hope that change means commitment to patient care, research, and an end to AIDS-related discrimination. I hope that change means reassessing our own attitudes towards friends and relatives (while they're still living). I hope that change means dedicating ourselves to optimism, rather than giving into the pessimism of our worst fears. And I hope that change lasts long after the final name panel need be read. Let the Quilt become again what it was meant to be: A living memorial to those who have died and a testament to our resolve to finally stitch in place the last Names panel.

Yes, the Quilt is beautiful. The Quilt is moving, and certainly, the Quilt does represent our response to a frustration we cannot currently conquer. But the Quilt should not become a representation of secular ritual and pageantry, and it should not merely function as a monument to Death.

I pray that someday that Quilt will grow no larger. I pray that it will serve as but a reminder of the terrible era of which we are all a part. Until that day arrives, let the Quilt represent our resolve to seeing that no one else dies of the plague that has claimed so many of our friends.

Section Three:
On Being Gay in the Real World

Twenty One
A Heterosexual Questionnaire

Over the years, social scientists have studied the complex questions of gay sexual orientation in great depth. In fact, it's difficult to be openly gay for very long without being asked to fill out questionnaires and surveys concerning the hows, whys, and wherefores of gay sexual identity.

As gays and lesbians, we are besieged with a multitude of seemingly innocent questions, designed to discover the physiological and psychological components that come together to form what is called the gay personality.

Who among us has not been asked questions such as: When did you first discover you were homosexual? Isn't it possible that your homosexuality is just a phase you might outgrow? Could it be that what you really need is a well-practiced heterosexual lover?

The questions are usually generated out of ignorance and misunderstanding, but that's the way it is with things not understood. Given that homosexuality has been hidden deep in the closet, away from the mainstream of contemporary society for so long, it isn't surprising that straight people want to know the secrets of what they consider our mysterious and aberrant lifestyle. To the average straight person, the very thought of homosexuality provokes a series of disturbing questions and concerns that confuse the living daylights out of their secure, pedestrian little worlds. For many of them, it is downright threatening to think that there could actually be people who are happy, secure, and proud of their gay identity. For most non-gays, being gay is an enigma of sexual acceptability; a threatening reality that challenges their own sexual identity, and one with which they would rather not deal.

Gays and lesbians are a societal anomaly. We don't fit accepted familial norms. We confound the church, confuse medical and psychological practitioners, and threaten to disrupt political stability. In fact, no other subculture within the forced melting pot of American society generates as much confusion, hatred, disgust, fear, and ill temper as does homosexuality.

The seemingly innocent questions asked by overly zealous researchers, provoke behavioral investigation that boarders on orientation genocide. Historically, research concerning the issue of homosexuality has been structured on a medical/psychological model, which purports that if causation could only be isolated to several common variables, then a cure could be more easily discovered. Only recently have gay and lesbian researchers been successful in halting the onslaught of empirical genocide by investigating homosexuality for the purposes of more clearly understanding the gay identity as it is, and for chronicling the everyday life experiences of gay men and women, not for the purpose of finding a cure!

Since I really don't care to be investigated by non-gay researchers in their attempt to alter my aberrant, promiscuous, emotionally disturbed behavior, I have adapted a questionnaire originated by Dr. Martin Rochlin that proposes a series of questions that we as gays and lesbians can put to our non-gay counterparts in the hope of discovering the causation of their vile and disgusting behavior. We've been asked these same questions for years; now it's their turn.

What do you think caused your heterosexuality?

When and how did you first decide your were a practicing heterosexual?

Is it possible that your heterosexuality is just a phase you might outgrow?

Is it possible that your heterosexuality stems from a neurotic fear of people of the same sex?

Isn't it possible that all you need is a well-practiced gay lover to turn your life around?

Heterosexuals have histories of failure in gay relationships. Do you think you may have turned to heterosexuality out of a fear of rejection?

If you've never slept with a person of the same sex, how do you know you wouldn't prefer that?

If heterosexuality is normal, why are a disproportionate number of mental patients heterosexual?

To whom have you disclosed your heterosexual tendencies? How did they react?

Your heterosexuality doesn't offend me as long as you don't try to force it on me. Why do you people feel compelled to seduce others into your heterosexual orientation?

Since ninety-three percent of child molesters are heterosexual, do you really consider it safe to expose your children to heterosexual teachers, coaches, etc.?

Why do you insist on being so obvious, and making a spectacle of yourself and your lifestyle? Do you have to flaunt your sexuality in the movies, on television, in magazines, and in public? Can't you just be what you are and keep it quiet?

Heterosexuals are noted for assigning themselves and each other narrowly restricted, stereotypical sex-roles. Why do you cling to such unhealthy role-playing?

How can you enjoy a fully satisfying sexual experience, or deep emotional rapport with a person of the opposite sex, when the obvious physical, biological, and temperamental differences between you are so vast?

Why do heterosexuals place such emphasis on sex?

With all the societal support that marriage receives, the divorce rate continues to spiral upward. Why do you think there are so few stable relationships among non-gay people?

Shouldn't you ask the far-out, straight types like fundamentalist Christians and right-wing ideologues to conform more? Wouldn't that improve your image?

There seems to be very few happy heterosexuals—drug and alcohol abuse, divorce, suicide, spousal and child abuse, and many other socially dysfunctional behaviors run rampant in the heterosexual community. Techniques have been developed that might allow you to change if you really want to. Have you considered behavioral modification therapy?

A disproportionate number of criminals, mental patients, skinheads, serial killers, and other irresponsible or anti-social types are heterosexual. Why would anyone want to hire a heterosexual for a responsible position?

Several years ago, heterosexual Marines stationed in the American Embassy in Russia were enticed into a sexual encounter with Russian women. Their behavior included group sex and rape, and then later they were blackmailed by the women. Doesn't this prove that non-gay people pose security risks to our country?

Single heterosexuals report having an alarming number of sexual partners. Why are heterosexuals so promiscuous?

Herpes, syphilis, and gonorrhea seem to have originated in the heterosexual community. Isn't that God's punishment for being straight? In fact, what about Sachs Syndrome in Jews, Sickle Cell Anemia in Blacks, Leukemia in young adults, or Alzheimer's disease in older adults? Is God punishing all of these people?

Do you and your partner adhere to specific roles when having sex? Is one of you passive and the other aggressive? Which one of you plays the male role and which one the female role?

Considering the menace that overpopulation presents, how could the human species survive if everyone were heterosexual?

How can you hope to become a whole person if you limit yourself to a compulsive, exclusive heterosexual choice and remain unwilling to explore and develop your natural, healthy God-given homosexual potential?

Ask your closest heterosexual friends or relatives to participate in your non-scientific, albeit interesting study, but don't expect any serious answers. After all, heterosexuals aren't accustomed to analyzing their own sexuality; they never have had to. In fact, most non-gays have given little thought to when, or why, or how they decided they were heterosexual. For them, most of these questions will come as a surprise and generate an uncomfortable challenge to their sexual identity—dangerous business for the gay researcher!

Rest assured, however, medical science is on your side. Recently, it was revealed that research has finally been able to trace the origination of heterosexuality back to as early as six months old. Scientists still haven't discovered which factors contribute to the development of the heterosexual psychosexual matrix, but take heart, because as soon as they do (and that day can't be very far off), a cure is sure to be found.

Twenty Two
The Two-Party Political System

A number of years ago, a popular radio comedian made famous a routine in which he mimicked a typical politician delivering a campaign speech. The comedian pontificated throughout the humorous speech, mumbling double-talk and nonsense, but appropriately punctuated his monologue with words such as America, the flag, God, and patriotism. On cue, the audience roared its approval, knowing all the while that the humorist was merely poking fun at the empty rhetoric of politicians, and everyone laughed, not only at the humor, but at the issue it satirized.

The two major political parties stage increasingly unpopular conventions every four years to anoint presidential candidates that mirror one another's middle-of-the road politics. This has always been a rich source for humor.

The Democrats convene first, usually during the summer, to crown the survivor of their primary slugfest, and, soon after, the Republicans meet to select their empty-promise-presidential candidate. But who gets the nomination from each party often doesn't matter, for they are virtually clones of one another, and neither candidate truly intends to lead the country in any particular direction other than straight down the status quo road.

Despite campaign promises about conservative ideology or progressive unity, elected presidents cater—for the most part—to the middle-of-the road masses (after all, a second term in office demands moving towards the center).

Presidential nominating conventions used to provide good-old-boy, back-room, pork-barrel electioneering, but not anymore—not in this enlightened day and age. Now, we voters have a significant voice in determining who wins each party's nomination, and, long before the first convention delegates step off the plane and head for the nearest bar in the host convention city, we know who the dismal candidates will be.

Indeed, the conventions aren't what they used to be. And that's good; at least now we voters have a say in selecting the presidential candidates, but there just doesn't seem to be anything beneficial about the method of contemporary candidate selection. It reeks of big money and special interests.

But take heart! There is always the possibility that single interest groups like the Right to Life, the National Rifle Association, The Christian Right, Citizens for a Decent America, or People-Against-Everything-and-Everyone-Unlike-Themselves might disrupt the proceedings with demands for the inclusion of a specific agenda in one or both of the major party platforms (not that anyone pays attention to the platforms after the election).

And so the chicanery of political buffoonery continues amidst the red, white, and blue of balloons, buttons, bumper stickers, and worthless campaign verbiage. But, you know what is really frightening about the whole ridiculous nonsense? You know what is truly unfortunate about the time, money, and energy spent in political hooliganism? You know what is genuinely unnerving about the whole tired charade of two-party politics? It's that despite the lack of substance on the part of the candidates, regardless of the voluminous platform language, and in spite of convention rhetoric, nothing will significantly alter (barring an invasion by a foreign country) the way we Americans work, think, feel, live, or die.

It doesn't matter which party is elevated to the Presidency—things won't change significantly. It doesn't matter what the party platforms espouse—they will be tossed out like yesterday's news as soon as the election results cool. It doesn't matter how many inflated phrases will echo throughout the convention halls—little will be done to help the poor, feed the hungry, save the environment, cure the sick, prevent crime, end war, enact universal health care, make solvent social security, or extend equal rights to oppressed citizens. And, unfortunately, that seems acceptable to the majority of citizens who even bother to vote. We've been convinced that the most effective course to pursue is middle road mediocrity; the good old Yankee Doodle Dandy system of two-party political patronage.

We early twenty-first century Americans hate the thought of change. We deplore anything new, anything different—we fear the unknown and our politicians know it. They feed upon our insecurities and take their cues from us. They embrace the way they think we want them to be, because after all, that's the only way to get elected in November. Both major parties mirror the loss of direction that defined American society in the early twentieth century and both reflect the same fears that carried us through the end of that millennium.

Despite all we hear about critical social issues, the voters, the politicians, and most of all, the defenders of the two-party system will perpetuate the chicanery of politics as usual. Why give up power that is equally traded back and forth in the Executive and Legislative branches of government? Although slogans and promises might change from time to time, as do political party winners, the reality of power continues to rest with those who make the rules to benefit only the two-party system and exclude all other contenders for the throne.

The state of current politics is sad commentary on the ideas envisioned by our forebears. What it has become is little better than a rubber stamp agreement between both parties. Our political heroes feed us campaign baloney in the form of patriotic rhetoric, television sound bites, and generalized media over-exposure—all in the name of democracy.

But worst of all, we listen—to the same worn-out, nonsense politicians and jump to our feet when we hear words like America, God, tax cuts, balanced budget, health care, and social security reform spill from their calculating mouths. For some reason, we cling to the myth that the two-party system actually works, that there really is a difference between a Republican and a Democrat. Well, check it out. Take a long, hard look at recent history.

Regardless of the party in power, little has seriously changed. African Americans have yet to achieve their long overdue freedom. Women have yet to gain economic, social, and political equality with men. Gay men and lesbians still are treated unequally under the law. We still have the poor among us. There are still far too many under- and unemployed workers. Children continue to go to sleep hungry. We have yet to extend universal health care to all of our citizens. Our environment continues to deteriorate. Terrorism still threatens our safety. Homeless Americans are still sleeping on the streets of our cities. And crime and drugs continue to keep us prisoners in our homes.

It's not that America is such a bad place to live; we still harbor the promise of hope, success, and charity for all. But we have to purge ourselves of the belief that politicians will save us. We have to eliminate the notion that what they say is what we will get. And we have to analyze more carefully than ever their every word and promise.

There are many opportunities to change the United States through political means, but the choices do not necessarily rest with the powers-that-be. We have been led to believe that we are historically a two-party system, but to the contrary, our early history was one of no party government—government by caucus, as a matter of fact. America emerged as a two-party system only after the Federalists, Anti-Federalists, Jeffersonians, and Jacksonians weakened into the current two-party system of government. Our history is actually ripe with examples of third and fourth party successes, but most have been relegated to the back pages of history, or are regarded as inconsequential, era-specific phenomena. Interestingly, the alternative parties worked—for a while—because people voted their conscience and not party loyalty.

Think about that the next time you vote. There are other political parties and candidates from whom to select: the National Alliance Party, the Taxpayers Party, the Libertarian Party, the Socialist Workers Party, the American Independent Party, United We Stand, the Green Party, and the Natural Law Party, to name just a few. There is more to a presidential election than the two, tired political retreads that the Republicans and the Democrats offer up.

At a dinner appearance several years ago, openly gay Congressman Barney Frank of Massachusetts told an attentive audience that voting for a particular candidate did not mean that one was endorsing that politician's entire philosophy. Frank claimed that voters were simply selecting the right person, for the right job, given the specific moment.

Truth be, Frank's advice was motivated out of a self-serving interest in supporting his state's governor (then Presidential candidate, Michael Dukakis), even at the chagrin of gays and lesbians in his home district. What Frank was saying was: Vote the party line, even if you don't agree with the candidate's philosophies. Once again, the same old political rhetoric. And this from an openly gay congressman.

For the past several elections, voters have been forced into choosing between what we sadly refer to as the lesser of two evils, not a very attractive position in which to be. But it is the two-party system and the rhetorical hogwash of politicians that have gotten us into this mess. Why should we expect them to lead us out? Only we—the voters—can get ourselves out, and now is as good a time as ever.

Your ballot is more than simply a choice between the two major parties. In fact, your decision will help shape the direction of the United States in the twenty-first century. Surely, we can do better than simply selecting between the lesser of two evils. Surely we have bigger dreams. Surely we really do care about ourselves, our country, and each other more than giving in to fear, as current politicians would have us do.

Good grief, I hope so anyway!

Twenty Three
One Part Gay, One Part War

I have been told by several people in the G/L/B/T press that the invasion of Iraq and the overthrow of Saddam Hussein have little to do with the gay community, and, therefore, should receive minimal attention from gays and lesbians. I fear such an attitude is shortsighted. War can be defined in no more pleasant terms than exactly what it is—war, complete with death, destruction, and horror. I can't help thinking that ignoring a national, indeed a world event of the magnitude of war and claiming that it doesn't concern our community portends a narrow view of the world politic.

Regardless of how each of us feels about the policies that led to war in Iraq, we can't pretend that it isn't happening. Some have decried President Bush's hasty rush to war; others have endorsed his actions with little apprehension; while still others believe that the United States has no business (other than economic—oil, that is) in the Middle East to begin with. To assume that war doesn't affect our community presumes a one-dimensional view that begs the proverbial head in the sand mentality. Gay men and lesbians have been called upon to fight, some have been taken prisoner, and too many (one is too many) have returned home in a body bag. How can we claim that *any* war does not affect us?

We have long argued that, in similar proportion to the general population, ten to fifteen percent of the U.S. military is gay and lesbian. It is fair, then, to assume that the same percentage of those fighting and dying will be gay or lesbian. Simple battlefield arithmetic adds credence to the demand for the equal disposition of gays and lesbians in military service.

With the invasion of Iraq, for the first time since Vietnam (other than "police" actions such as the invasions of Panama and Grenada, involvement in Somalia and Bosnia, and the first Persian Gulf War), gays and lesbians have been expected to suffer the horrors of war, and yet, still have been denied the right to serve their country openly and with pride.

Before the war began, a Pentagon spokesman admitted that, although gays and lesbians would be expected to "do their duty," they would be ignominiously booted from military service once the conflict had been resolved. In other words, the government of the United States is willing to use us as pawns on the battlefield, only to kick us out of the service once hostilities are over. Such policy reflects the typical mentality of dictatorial control over minorities who are regarded as little more than sacrificial lambs to the slaughter. But should we be surprised? Hardly. The same type of policy was used against African Americans even up through the police action in Korea in the early 1950s. Dare we disregard this duplicitous hypocrisy?

If the occupation of Iraq drags on for an extended length of time, as some experts predict, more and more gay men and lesbians will be called upon to do their duty—secretly, of course. We then would not only see the call to service of volunteers and reservists, but even possibly the conscription of young men and women for whom war is just a television drama away. Consider the drain on the gay organizations that are dominated by younger adults, the decreased numbers available for our fight for domestic equality, and the shift in attention away from liberation issues. Our ranks will be depleted, our struggle threatened, our cause weakened. And what is even more ironic is that gays and lesbians will be expected to fight for the freedom of people in places thousands of miles beyond our national boarders, while still being denied those same rights here at home.

Don't ask...don't tell. Can we still argue that war—any war—is not our issue too? What about funding for AIDS research, the homeless, the environment, family issues, gay marriage, or any one of a score of other domestic concerns that stir the conscience of both ours and the majority communities. Undoubtedly, a prolonged occupation will siphon tax dollars away from a social agenda and funnel it into the military. The focus of government will naturally shift to war and away from the issues that define domestic progress such as reduced funding for important research, narrowed national foci, diminished resources—indeed, legitimate concerns of every American.

Like it or not, we gays are still citizens of the United States, and as such, we too go to war when our country goes to war. Some may argue that by being denied equality, our responsibility to country is abrogated. But such logic is irrelevant in the case of war, for the argument concerning the effect war has upon our community does not demand the posturing of advocacy or disapproval. Accepting citizenship does not imply tacit approval of the policies of war. We are still free to agree or not, to support or dissent, but we are still called upon to serve.

What our attention does demand, however, is that we not ignore war as not being a G/L/B/T issue, for the pawns that innocently execute policy will ultimately come from our community, as well as the general community. In war many suffer and some will die, and that places war at the very doorstep of not only our community, but in every community, city, town, and burg in the United States.

It is perilous to ignore history as it is being written; illogical to neglect the redefinition of geopolitics; and naïve to disregard economic, political, and social change that will shape not only the future of this nation, but also of our community. We are not a people of tunnel vision. We must reach beyond that which we regard as gay and lesbian and accept our place as members of the larger society. Is this not that for which we have long struggled? How, then, dare we pretend that war does not affect us?

One can hardly watch death explode from the televisions in our homes and not be affected. Emotions become strained, sensitivities dulled, and sentiment confused. We vacillate between elation and despair, patriotism and shame, confidence and doubt. At times we find ourselves cheering the kills of war, at other times cursing the intransigence that caused battle. Such emotions are natural to the catastrophe of war. It is understandable to feel this strange hypocrisy—one day decrying political policy and the next hoping for victory. Such is the oppressive psychology of war; such is its insidious horror.

As is the case with all citizens of the United States, gays and lesbians will lose friends and family in war—that makes it our issue. As is the case with all citizens of the United States, gays and lesbians will be called upon to serve and fight in war—that makes it our issue. As is the case with other minorities who are discriminated against, then used as pawns in someone else's war, gays and lesbians will be used as fodder for the fight—that makes it our issue. The reality of war is that it is larger than a single battle, an individual action, or a struggle the magnitude of all-out hostilities. We cannot pretend that issues that so directly and severely affect the G/L/B/T community do not affect us, also, as citizens of the country in which we live.

There is no doubt that governmental policy, such as being discharged from the military because a person is gay or lesbian, must be vigorously opposed. Unquestionably, the scraps of bone former President Clinton tossed us with his Don't ask...don't tell policy must be challenged at every level. And there is an honest argument to be made for opposing all wars for reasons of humanitarian principle. But we cannot simply turn our backs when war does happen and pretend it does not affect us.

We are citizens of this world and, as such, we suffer war as does all humankind. We fear, we tremble, and we weep. Were we to deny this reality, then surely would we repudiate our sensitivity, clearly would we forfeit our humanity, and certainly would we reject the spirit that makes us a gentle, loving people.

War is a G/L/B/T issue, not because we rally to a chorus of blind patriotism, but rather because war's reality will redefine our struggle for equality, reshape our place in the world, redirect our resources and attention away from issues of domestic concern, and ultimately change each and every one of us as individuals. Let us hope that we can shed the obstinacy that narrows our vision and accept the responsibility that demands a community of people look beyond its single interest.

Whether it be war in the Middle East or anywhere else on this planet—war is brutal, deadly, and destructive, and denying our involvement, simply because we want to pretend otherwise, is ignorant. War is hell, and given the horror that it causes and the change that it brings—not only to the world community, but to our own—it is, without question, a gay and lesbian issue.

Twenty Four
What Family Values?

The Christian Right, that combination of extreme right-wing conservatism and Evangelical Christianity, has it all wrong. I'm sick and tired of hearing the fundamentalist new right, conservative garbage spill from the mouths of those holier-than-thou pontificators who think they know what American life should be like. Their most recent political buzz-phrase (made popular during the Reagan presidency and continuing today), focuses upon their interpretation of a return to good old American, Christian family values, whatever the heck that means!

Consider the words that make up the interpretation of the phrase. First, *American*. Who among the Christian Right has the right to determine what is American? This is a nation derived from diverse cultures, nationalities, races, ethnicities and religions. Being American means recognizing and respecting the cultures of Africa, Asia, Europe, Latin America, and Native America. Dare we define American as being subject only to white, Anglo-Saxon Protestant morality? The Christian Right would have us think so.

What about the word *Christian* in the phrase? There are many sects and denominations of Christianity. Which one defines the true representation of that religion? Are we talking about Methodist, Baptist, Lutheran, Episcopalian, the Assembly of God, Presbyterian, or the new wave of evangelicals, fundamentalists, Pentecostals, and so on? Historically, the Roman Catholic Church tried to establish itself as the One Church, but now we have to deal, not only with its hypocrisy, but with varying Biblical interpretations preached by scores more denominations. Given that Christianity has no one center of theological determination, it is ludicrous to suppose the existence of such a thing as universal Christian interpretation.

How about the term *family values*? That's a good one—let's return to good old family values. Of course the model for those so-called good old days rests with one of two interpretations. One reverts back to a pre-World War II era when men were in complete control. Women and children were their property, women had virtually no divorce or inheritance rights, male against female spousal abuse was legal, and children were produced for the purpose of greasing the economic concept of human capital. Now that sounds all-American in an enlightened age of equality and human rights!

The other interpretation refers to the fictional tripe of 1950s and '60s television Americana: Ozzie and Harriet, Ricky and Dave; Ward and June, Wally and the Beav; Alex and Donna Stone, Mary and Jeff; Jim Anderson and his Springfield brood; and in the seventies and early eighties, the Partridge Family and the Brady Bunch.

Let's see: Mom stayed home, bore the children, tended house, raised the kids, gossiped with neighboring wives, and got messed up in some harebrained scheme that dear old Dad had to resolve after coming home from a long, tiring day at the office.

Dad went to work (but what he did was never revealed) and brought home the bacon (cholesterol had yet to be identified as a health risk in those days), always wore a suit and tie (even when cutting the grass), doled out wisdom and discipline at a rate that would make King Solomon jealous, occasionally played penny-ante poker with the guys, and showed emotion and sensitivity only when the situation called for it. Of course much to Mom's chagrin, Dad never helped around the house—that's what kids were for!

Naturally, the kids excelled at school, with the exception of the occasional spit-ball-at-the-teacher incident, which was neatly resolved in 23 minutes, never thought about drugs or alcohol, went to the sock hop on Friday night, dated Betty Lou or Bud and were always around to help Mom with the housework, reluctantly of course, but ever so dutifully and lovingly.

Sounds idyllic. What we didn't hear about in television America was Dr. Stone's affair with Harriet, Ozzie's illegal tax write-offs, Jeff and Ricky out behind the garage smoking and doing the nasty, Betty Anderson secretly off to New York for an illegal abortion, and Kitten (remember cute little Cathy Anderson), hawking dope at the neighborhood Junior High. In other words, there were problems then too, but they weren't portrayed for a variety of reasons, which resulted in the appearance of the United States as family perfect.

What the Christian Right means when they say we should return to those days of strong family values is that men should be in control. Women should be kept barefoot and silent, Dad's spousal possession. The kids should be seen and not heard and should only have problems like acne and which outfit to wear on the big date—and like women, should be little more than Dad's possessions. The whole family shouldn't be able to see reality beyond the ends of their pug little noses.

Good old family values are really all about: control, domination, and mindless subservience. There weren't such things as racism, ageism, sexism, homophobia, spousal abuse, child abuse, rape, drug and alcohol abuse, environmental pollution, crime, and poverty in 1950s television-land. Those things were conveniently swept under the rug in an Eisenhowerian belief in America's being the strongest and most economically powerful nation on Earth. Women listened to their men, children did what they were told, and men controlled everything—look where that's gotten us!

When people say we should return to good old American family values, they usually don't know what they are talking about. *Family values* means little more than nostalgia being foisted upon the public as a result of frustration with the social problems of contemporary American life, interestingly most of which took root in the good old days of family values. Although nostalgia might be fun for a theme party, it doesn't represent reality. What it does is capitalize on the best of the times, while conveniently forgetting the worst of the times. Charles Dickens had it right!

The concept of family began in pre-historic times as a means of procreation, protection, and security—it had nothing to do with contemporary ideals of romanticized love. It evolved during Biblical times as a unit for the convection of family name (i.e., the man's name) and inheritance. There wasn't such a thing as sanctified marriage—male/female coupling was an agreement arranged by the elders of the tribes for the purpose of establishing social order and tribal autonomy and was actuated by tribal ritual. The men were often afforded a choice in their women, but the women were pandered (without choice) as property; and the couple's offspring were little more than possessions.

In feudal times, the concept of family continued such that a man took a wife, not out of love, but for the purpose of legalizing family names and inheritance for his legitimate offspring (as opposed to the other children he had fathered out of wedlock, but who of course, had no legal, social, or religious rights). Eventually, the Christian Church blessed such unions and encouraged legal partners to reproduce for the purpose of augmenting tribal and religious populations. Nothing wrong with swelling the numbers for potential tribal, religious, or nationalistic war! Besides, granting marriage decrees meant money in a church's coffers.

The concept of passing legal name and inheritance continued throughout the Middle Ages, and into the eighteenth and nineteenth centuries and eventually into colonial America, with women still being regarded as possessions, and children as human capital. Not until well into the twentieth century were there laws to protect wives or children from the abuse and oppression of husbands and fathers.

The contemporary concept of the loving family came to fruition in mid-twentieth century America with Hollywood and television representations of romanticized love, and Hallmark's invention of card-giving holidays like Mother's Day and Father's Day, Grandparent's Day, and Sweetest Day. Our "Christian" nation even panders to the pre-Christian customs of Halloween and St. Valentine's Day that have been sanitized into Christian ritual and belief. The reality is that good old American Christian family values means domination, ownership, and possession by men; and subservience, oppression, and second-class citizenship for women and children (and minorities, who were, of course, considered a part of the good old days for purposes of subservience and comic relief—ah yes, the minstrel show).

Here's a better idea, and this should please the Christian Right. If we're going to return to something vaguely labeled as the good old days, why not take it all the way and return to the days of proto-man, when the male went out, clubbed his woman over the head, dragged her back to the cave, and did whatever it was that cavemen did to cavewomen. That should eliminate all the social problems we have in twenty-first century America. Let's not go forward—today's evangelical leaders would never stand for that—let's regress! Male power, domination, and possession all rolled into one—what a perfect combination!

Or we could learn to respect individuals and groups for who they are and extend them the unalienable rights supposedly guaranteed by the Constitution: equality and opportunity. Further, we could emphasize what is supposed to be the American ideal of respect and honor for everyone. What a novel idea. Not very good-old-American-Christian-fundamentalist-right-wing oriented family values, but certainly revolutionary.

Twenty Five
Gay Marriage, Civil Unions, and the Destruction of Civilization As We Know It

I am gay and if I were in love at this particular time in twenty-first century America, I couldn't get married if I wanted to. Of course I could motor off to Massachusetts and tie the knot, but my marriage wouldn't be recognized in any other state in the union—like heterosexual marriages are. Or I could go north of the boarder to Canada, where gay marriages are legally recognized, but that wouldn't matter. Down here in rightwing-land, foreign blessed unions are not accepted either. In fact, other than a handful of states that recognize gay/lesbian marriage, civil unions, or legal spousal rights there is nowhere for me to go in the United States, legally, if I want to openly and religiously declare my love for my partner. And if you ask me—that is a sin of Biblical proportions.

According to moralists intent on denying gays and lesbians complete equality, if we were allowed to marry, we'd destroy the sanctity of the holy heterosexual institution of marriage as we know it (and we'd probably bring down all of civilization, as we know it, at the same time). Think about the illogic for a moment: heterosexuals who oppose our rights to marry—or at the least enter into a legal civil union—on the one hand regard gays and lesbians as abnormal, sinful creatures, while on the other hand assume we have the power to destroy the historical institution of marriage. Sounds like we're far more powerful than I thought! Of course, the same people would, likely, argue that evil—like gays—is rampant in the world and we're simply the minions of Satan out to confuse and entice the innocent into a world of debauchery. In the end, we're either terribly powerful innocents who scare the heck out of a significant percentage of heterosexuals, or we're in bed with the Devil, himself, plotting the downfall of Christianity, the United States, and all of Western Civilization. Wow!

As far as statistics go, at this point in time, only six states recognize any form of gay coupling. Massachusetts has legalized gay marriage, Vermont and Connecticut have passed legislation to acknowledge civil unions, and Hawaii, Maine, New Jersey, and California have differing laws that allow for spousal-like rights or near spousal-like rights for gays and lesbians. That leaves forty-four states that have either passed legislation, referendums, or constitutional amendments prohibiting the rights of gays and lesbians to participate in the same institution that heterosexuals have been permitted to enjoy for thousands of years.

Intellectually, however, the issue of gay/lesbian marriage isn't one of statistics, but rather one of equal rights. Mere numbers don't begin to tell the story of why we are being denied the same civil liberty that heterosexuals are allowed. Were you to listen to the ranting from the far right—and unfortunately, Middle America has been sucked into their illogical rhetoric, too—you would hear that marriage is a sanctified, religious union between a man and a woman only; a concept most recently popularized by the George W. Bush's administration attempt to constitutionally define marriage as specifically excluding gays and lesbians.

But of course the issue goes far beyond the officious prattling of George W. He has many allies who have both preceded his contempt for gays, or who have jumped on his holier-than-thou bandwagon. The currently popular Defense of Marriage Act, political pontificating, and pandering to the political religious right are the three main issues standing in the way of gays, lesbians and marriage. And none of them make the least bit of sense.

Consider, first, The Defense of Marriage Act. I'm curious, someone help me out here. Why does marriage need to be defended? Are gays and lesbians attacking it? Are we trying to bring it down and destroy the very concept of lifelong partnership? Is there something I don't know about our nefarious attempt to blind-side Western Civilization? I thought that when two people, regardless of their sexual orientation, agreed to enter into a religiously blessed, holy union, in the sight of God, family, friends, and witnesses, they would be glorifying the act of marriage—not attacking it!

Attacking it...hardly.

Look at the facts. Over fifty percent of heterosexual marriages end in divorce; only about seven percent of gay or lesbian couples who have been together for five years or longer end in separation. Figure it out for yourself; use your intelligence. Which of those two groups seems more detrimental to marriage—the group with a plus fifty percent divorce rate, or the group with a minimal seven percent separation rate?

Research demonstrates that a significant percentage of heterosexuals participate in what sociologists call serial monogamy—that is moving from one marriage relationship to another: get married, file for divorce, get married again, file for divorce, get married a third time, file for divorce, ad infinitum. The same research indicates that committed gay or lesbian relationships are appreciably more permanent; thus nullifying the contemporary concept of serial monogamy. I fully realize that these statistics—for both heterosexuals and homosexuals do not apply to singles, or couples that get together on a whim. We're talking about individuals who have made a serious, lifelong commitment to one another, not the promiscuity and adultery that is rampant in both the heterosexual and homosexual populations.

Consider, also, the rearing of children—a point frequently addressed by those opposed to homosexual marriage. Raising children is the province of heterosexuals, many argue, that is best suited for a man and a woman only (of course this conveniently ignores the issue of heterosexual, single-parent families—a phenomenon that is dramatically redefining the concept of "family" in contemporary America). Again, research overwhelmingly indicates that gay or lesbian couples who raise children rear them to be less violent, more accepting of people different from themselves, better psychologically adjusted, and who perform better in school, in sports, and in ancillary school activities. Wow, that surely is a serious blow to gay marriage and the demands associated with raising children!

What about the argument I've heard enumerated by people who oppose gay marriage—that gay and lesbian couples probably wouldn't fit into a predominantly heterosexual neighborhood; they would be social pariahs in a straight bastion of suburbia. Again, research demonstrates that heterosexual couples who live in neighborhoods with homosexual couples report that all couples participate equally in the bonding rituals common to middle-class American life: block parties, yard sales, baby sitting, house-watching while one couple is away on an extended trip, and so on. Straight and gay couples report virtually no problems living together in mixed neighborhoods. Seems to be no problem there, either.

What about spousal abuse in heterosexual marriages? Virtually unheard of in gay or lesbian unions. How about child abuse within the family? Again, effectively non-existent with gay and lesbian couples. What about the reportedly significant occurrence of adultery in heterosexual marriages? Again, all but absent in gay and lesbian couplings.

When the evidence is taken into consideration, it appears that gay and lesbian couples aren't a threat to marriage at all; in fact, queer couples seem to take the institution of marriage more seriously than do many heterosexual couples.

Second, consider the plethora of political pontificating. That's an easy issue with which to dispense. The history of our country is endemic with scaremongers who jump on any bandwagon just to get reelected, or to appease a minority percentage of their constituency. Our nation's history has been rife with those who promoted slavery, who insisted women were not intelligent enough to vote, who wagged their fingers (and tongues) at interracial couples and marriage, and more recently, politicos who would have us believe that Islamic terrorists are preparing to march into our individual homes and slaughter our entire families if we don't listen to their frightful warnings. It goes on and on. Grab on to an issue that frightens people and someone is bound to listen.

Scare the voters enough so they'll march to the ballot box and cast their trembling vote for the demagogue of the week and you're sure to enlist a following. During the depths of the Great Depression, Franklin Delano Roosevelt proclaimed in his first inaugural address "...that the only thing we have to fear is fear itself." It seems that some of today's politicians would have us believe that we have nothing to fear except...everything! And gays and lesbians are one of those "things" to fear—especially if they want to get married.

Third, consider the pandering to religion. I am fully aware that some God-fearing Christians will point out any number of passages from scripture that state that marriage is only to be enacted between a man and a woman. But if one were to examine the concept of marriage during Biblical times, one would discover that marriage was a profoundly different institution than it is today.

Women and men did not fall in love and get married, as we do now. A woman was property, betrothed to a man in an arrangement that benefited primarily the man's family with a dowry and continuity through the expected children. The benefit to the woman's family was that they no longer had to bear the expense and care of an unmarried daughter. Also, if you could marry your daughter to someone higher up in the social hierarchy, your family could perhaps become cozy with the families that controlled tribal activity.

The only choice a woman had was to marry whoever had been selected for her. In fact, if one were to study the history of marriage, one would discover that marriages during the time surrounding the life of Christ were not blessed by God, as is the practice today, but were entered into as civil ceremonies to control community or tribal wealth, unity, and continuity. Many Christians are unaware that Mary the Mother of Jesus Christ was betrothed to Joseph at a very young age, and protested vehemently to her cousins that she did not want to marry him.

They didn't walk down an aisle with ring bearers and flower girls, happily proclaiming their love for one another.

Throughout most of history and the entire world, marriage has been entered into for the purpose of producing legal offspring for the purpose of continuing the family name, legalizing male inheritance, and providing for the continuation of property, ownership, title, and tribal position. Certainly there are exceptions to this historical reality, but for the most part the reasoning behind marriage was exceedingly practical.

It wasn't until the Roman Catholic Church seized control of the crumbling Roman Empire that marriage became sanctified in the name of God—and that was for the purpose of raising money for the church, controlling the population, and advancing theological belief—not for the purpose of initiating a holy union. For the most part, women remained the property of their husbands. A husband was legally permitted to beat his wife, father children out of wedlock, and divorce or kill his wife if she did not meet his husbandly needs (e.g., the production of sufficient male offspring).

The concept of marriage eventually evolved into what it is today, after centuries of male dominance, female subservience, and maneuvering by men who controlled religion, politics, familial issues, tribal concerns, and virtually everything having to do with legal affairs. Now—meaning in the more recent history of the modern world—marriage has developed into what we know it as today: a blessed union between a man and a woman for the purpose of glorifying God and raising children.

So much for the wonderful history of marriage, political pontificating, and the Defense of Marriage Act.

Curiously, the social institutions that could help in lobbying for gay marriage, civil unions, spousal benefits, and civil liberties for gays and lesbians might be economics, business, and the corporate world. More and more companies, both large and small, are extending spousal benefits to same-sex couples. Given the number of corporations that do business, or have offices in multiple states, it will become increasingly difficult for those companies to offer same-sex benefits, if a particular state in which they do business prohibits such rights by legislation, referendum, or constitutional amendment. Such a prohibition is apt to discourage any particular company from operating branch offices and/or factories in those states and to negatively affect the transfer of gay and lesbian employees from one state to another. If this situation were to evolve, it could backfire on the gay-restrictive states as they lose tax revenue or fail to develop a stronger business climate as corporations move their investments into more gay-friendly states.

One might argue that such a scenario is unlikely, given the reluctant history of corporate America to lobby for African American and women's rights, but it is not an impossibility. What an irony for the gay and lesbian community if support from corporate America were the impetus in advancing our cause, when its past history has been one of discrimination against gays and lesbians. Still, the G/L/B/T community must look for support from every possible venue. We are at a crossroads in our struggle for equality of all kinds—marriage, civil unions, spousal benefits, and specifically equal rights under the law—and we dare not close our doors to those who would assist in our struggle, whether it be motivated out of what is right and ethical, or simply what is economic and good for business.

This still leaves us with the issue of gay marriage in twenty-first century America as damned by social moralists. Is there some reason why some heterosexuals are afraid to share marriage rights with gays and lesbians? Do they fear we might end up sharing in the same legal amenities, obligations, and responsibilities they enjoy? Are they afraid we might get to file federal, state, and local income taxes as a couple, rather than as individuals? And do they forget that marriage means not only enjoying the benefits of a coupled situation, but accepting the responsibilities and obligations, thereof. If two gay men or two lesbians are willing to accept the entirety of marriage—including both the positives and the negatives—why then do they pose a threat to the institution? It seems that such an arrangement would do nothing more than strengthen the institution of marriage.

When a heterosexual man and woman marry, they are permitted a number of rights that same-sex couples are denied by law. Married couples can file joint tax returns—gay and lesbian couples cannot. Married couples have unquestioned visitation rights when one member of the couple is hospitalized—gay and lesbian couples do not. Married couples can make medical decisions for an incapacitated spouse—gay and lesbian couples cannot, unless they obtain a power of attorney. Married couples can share the health benefits offered by private employers—gay and lesbian couples cannot, unless a specific company provides for spousal benefits. Married couples can adopt children—in most states, gay and lesbian couples cannot. In all fifty states, married couples enjoy the spousal benefits offered to state employees—gay and lesbian couples share in those benefits in only six states. Married couples have the right for the surviving mate to decide upon funeral arrangements—gay and lesbian couples do not. From A to Z, heterosexual married couples reap the bounty of marriage—gay and lesbian couples do not.

It is time we stopped pontificating, selectively interpreting the Bible to meet narrow-minded needs, and politicking based on fear. It is time we grew up and joined the other enlightened nations of this world that provide equal marriage treatment under the law for all, regardless of sexual orientation. It is time we searched our hearts and our souls for guidance. I cannot for a single moment believe that a God that would create me in Its image would then turn around and tell me, "Sorry, but you can't share in the same sacraments I give to my other children"!

If I want to spend fifty years loving, living with, caring for, growing old with, and burying the man I love, then whose business is it other than his and mine. It is our choice to make with the love and guidance from the God we would ask to bless our holy union. Is that so bad? Does that threaten marriage? Dare that portend the end of civilization as we know it?

I think not.

Twenty Six
A Need for Urgency

As we head into a new century, I am reminded of an oft-repeated, but appropriate expression that has come to be used as a call to vigilance by the champions of social justice. The phrase "Stand Up and Be Counted" sounds trite, but means so very much. It not only serves as a summons to social action, but encourages each person to take responsibility for one's dedication to the ideals that shape one's philosophy, and ultimately, one's life. The phrase is relevant, at this time in history, for the G/L/B/T community and warrants being repeated over and again. We must regard the twenty-first century as a time of action. We must—as gay men, lesbians, bisexuals, and transgendered people—stand up and be counted.

As we head into the new century, we leave behind two decades scored with much success and some failure. Certainly, the liberation movement progressed further during the 1980s and 1990s than it had during any previous time in American history, but near the end of the twentieth century, it became uncomfortably apparent that our cause was beginning to suffer a reversal of fortune.

A groundswell of negative reaction to gay marriage and civil unions, as well as setbacks in equal rights legislation seriously threatened to subvert the accomplishments of the previous twenty years. On the one hand, during the 1980s and 1990s a number of cities and several states throughout the country passed legislation that ensured civil rights and extended protection to gays and lesbians. The courts became more sensitive to our issues. Opinion polls showed that a growing majority of Americans supported our fight for equal rights. Churches relaxed dogmatic theology that had once condemned us as sinners, in favor of a more enlightened view of homosexual parishioners.

Throughout the country thousands of G/L/B/T political, social, recreational, and religious organizations sprang to life. We gained political power and prestige—even to the point of electing some of our own to public office. The once hostile media began reporting our issues and depicting us in ways that reflected reality, rather than pejorative myth, and in both 1987, and 1993, close to a million queers descended upon the nation's capitol in the largest human rights demonstrations in the history of the United States.

On the other hand, by century's end, gay bashing was still rampant and referendum voting had overturned many of the civil rights laws that had been enacted. Local courts began mimicking the conservatism of the U.S. Supreme Court. Churches began reversing their acceptance principle, in favor of theological fundamentalism. Gay marriage and civil unions became an excuse to exercise homophobia. Certainly, the last two decades of the twentieth century were the best of times and the worst of times for the G/L/B/T community.

As the movement's success of the 1980s devolved into the reversals of the 1990s and is now further degenerating in the early part of the twenty-first century, there are numerous anti-gay articles, editorials, and letters appearing in newspapers and on television throughout the country. Politicians have been given free rein to renew verbal gay bashing. The bigoted heterosexism of right-wing radio hosts can be heard in many cities and small town stations. The airwaves are choked with self-styled hate-mongers with huge listening audiences.

Although we live in a time when Christian, right-wing bigotry seems to have captured the imagination of the gullible public, we dare not succumb to fascist ideology. Even though we

Americans have been frightened back into the sanctuary of our homes because of crime and terrorism, we cannot acquiesce to fear. We still live in a time and a place that, if not providing for the equality of all people, continues to project the dream of the liberation of every person. This is not Nazi Germany, 1933. This is not Stalinist Russia, 1937. This is not Tiananmen Square, 1989. This is the United States of America, where hope, charity, and individual liberty are still championed as shared common values.

As we forge into the twenty-first century, we are presented with an opportunity to progress further and to redress the negative events and decisions that soured an otherwise successful generation, but we cannot do so without dedication and risk. We cannot do so without sacrifice and struggle. We cannot do so without courage and determination. It is time for gays, lesbians, bisexuals, and transgendered people everywhere to forsake the security of moderation and embrace the mantle of activism. It is time to stand up and be counted, for we cannot change that which needs changing until we are able to shed the apathy that threatens to consume us and shake the albatross of temperance from around our necks. Simply put, we must address the issues that keep us separated from the mainstream of American life.

First, we must increase the pressure on politicians to whom we have given our time, energy, and money. The day has long since passed when we should be content to help elect supportive legislators, and then shy away from demanding their action out of fear of offending them. The persons for whom we have worked are elected public servants—we and they must never forget that. Despite what some detractors might think, we deserve the attention and respect of those who have sought our support, then have abandoned us!

Second, political and social radicalism must continue, anew! To some people in this country, in both the general population and the G/L/B/T community, the concept of radicalism suggests confrontation and violence. To others, it means social revolution, and to still others it suggests anarchy. Whereas, in some instances, such approaches are essential to the liberation of our community, the true meaning of radicalism is experienced daily by every queer who dares live openly and honestly; proud of who and what he is, knowledgeable of her heritage, and insistent upon change—radical, sociopolitical change. We need not fear radicalism, for simply by living as open, out-of-the-closet fags, we are being radical. Status quo restraint will not secure our future. What we seek is equal treatment under the law, an end to discrimination, and the destruction of the heterosexist bias that prevents egalitarian evolution. If we were to be honest in addressing the reality of that for which we have long struggled, then that which we seek is revolution—not a blood bath of violence, but a peaceful and thorough transformation of society.

Third, we must redefine our methods and revitalize our approach to change. No longer can we afford to cling to the worn tactics of the 1980s and 1990s. Though such methods brought success, many have become dated and antiseptic. Parades, pride festivals, electioneering, staged media events, and $100 plate black-tie dinners have their place, but are used up and pale when contemplating what must be done. We must learn new skills, consider innovative ideas, utilize different methods, and implement inventive programs. We must use the non-gay media to our benefit by blanketing radio, television, and print with information campaigns. We must employ every outlet at our disposal and let our voice be heard throughout every corner of the country. We must reach not only the media, but our schools, churches, legislators, workplaces, and families and friends. We must speak loudly, but with sensibility. We must argue fiercely, but with compassion. We must educate, inform, and model until the ugly misunderstandings that surround homosexuality are finally, and at long last laid to rest.

Fourth, we must escape our self-imposed isolation and free ourselves of the deceit, self-hatred, and fear that accompanies living in solitude and fear. Certainly, coming out of the closet is a process best activated by the individual. No one dares tell another when he or she should come out, but neither should we discount the importance of personal regeneration that coming out encourages. Being out of the closet liberates us from imprisonment, it leads to self-acceptance and positive self-esteem, and it creates within each of us the ability to live as we were intended to—openly, honestly, and as contributing members of our society. We cannot achieve freedom as a community as long as we continue to isolate ourselves, individually. Coming out certainly involves risk—emotional, physical, and economic—but at the same time it releases us from doubt and self-pity. Until we all come out, we cannot expect the few to achieve victory for the many.

During the closing months of 1989, the world watched in amazement as the Iron Curtain lifted over Eastern Europe. We shed tears of joy as we observed millions of people tasting freedom for the first time. We cheered as the Berlin wall crumbled, applauded as liberation came in swift, monolithic change, delighted as hundreds of thousands poured into the streets demanding freedom and urging political transformation. Since the closing years of that decade, the world has continued to watch as country after country has been liberated from the cruelty of dictators and oppression. Countries in Europe, Asia, and Africa have joined the world community as independent, free nations.

The transformation in these countries seemed so simple, so quick, and so effective. Yet the brave individuals who faced their oppressors and demanded their rights risked their jobs, their homes, their families, and their lives with only a slim hope for success. But the risk worked because of their courage, determination, and dedication to their ideals. They shed the nightmare of oppression and are now free.

We in the G/L/B/T community are no different from our international friends. We continue to be oppressed, we remain captives to a system that values homogeneity and rejects diversity, and rest assured, our oppressors will not come to us with our freedom neatly secured for us. No one will grant us our civil rights simply because we exist. Few others will champion our cause when it threatens their own success.

We must accept responsibility for our own liberation, we must shape our own destiny, we must demand the protections guaranteed by the Constitution of the United States of America, and we must exact attention, insist upon equality, and settle for nothing less than total, unequivocal liberation.

The twenty-first century must be our century. If not now, when? We can no longer afford to wait. We can no longer accept third-class citizenship. We can no longer continue to live as social lepers in a world that is equally ours. We must seize the initiative and sound our message loudly and clearly and without hesitation.

Now is the time to make the commitment to social change. Now is the time we must pledge to work for political transformation. Now is the time we must dedicate ourselves to the struggle for which so many have sacrificed so much.

To the politicians who court our votes, then cowardly back away from championing our rights—the ballot box will undo your treachery.

To the conservative commentators who play on the insecurities of a frightened public and stir the cauldron of discontent—shame on you for pandering to misinformation and fear.

To the executives who produce Hollywood tripe and television garbage—shame on you for depicting gays and lesbians as comic relief and the 2000 version of black-face, minstrel shows.

To the print media that continues to publish right-wing intolerance and chauvinism—shame on you for abrogating your journalistic integrity.

To those who would rather see gays and lesbians remain third-class citizens in a country of hope and charity—shame on you for playing fast and loose with our constitutional rights.

To all the self-styled apologists of heterosexism—shame on you; be done and gone with your discrimination and hatred.

And to the G/L/B/T community, today is the time that we must accept our destiny, embrace our responsibilities, and stand up for what we believe.

Twenty Seven
That's All It Takes

Sometimes it takes a tragedy to put things into perspective. It shouldn't have to be that way, but that's the lot for us humans. Unintentionally, we become so wrapped up in our own lives that we tend to forget what is happening with our friends and families, we even forget what is happening in the world around us.

We forget that there are far worse things than the petty irritations we consider insurmountable. We think in terms of bad luck and too often pity ourselves for being the victims of circumstances beyond our control. We have a tendency to regard our own problems as monumental—the worst that things could possibly be! But of course, they really aren't that way at all.

It has happened to me. I fell victim to the poor-me syndrome when a problem developed that seemed beyond my control. Of course it wasn't, but I labored over my setback, nursed it like a festering wound, and coddled my shattered spirit as a child does a broken toy. I brooded and stewed, fussed and fumed, and worried myself into frenzy, wondering how I could possibly amend a situation that seemed absolutely unworkable.

Then, in March 2003, the United States went to war in Iraq and almost overnight, things were destined never to be the same again; not as much for me, but for millions of people in this country, in the Middle East, and around the world.

Suddenly, there were men and women dying, soldiers being taken captive, houses being bombed into oblivion, and lives being shattered all in the name of something we haven't yet been able to define. The euphoric burst of freedom that was seen in Eastern Europe from 1989 through the early 1990s had been abruptly dwarfed by the sounds and fury of war. People took positions, criticized those who disagreed with the prevailing sentiment, swelled with bloated patriotism, and demanded the death of people and nations for whom they had little understanding, or caring. Indeed, the New World Order that George Bush had long championed collapsed in the new presidency of his son George W.

Eventually, the world settles its bloody hostilities; it usually does—in one way or another, and to one side's satisfaction and the other's distress—but, we never seem to learn. Victories are won by the living, but soon to be dead. Battles are forgotten, the dead buried, and cities reborn in the comfortable span of a decade. But what the warring might mean for generations to follow will be tested by time and world events.

The incident concerning the invasion of Iraq started me thinking. Isn't it sad how we so often fail to see what's going on around us? We spend so much time worrying ourselves into apathy and ignoring the reality of life, that we don't look beyond ourselves to see the suffering of others.

I like to think of myself as a sensitive, caring person; it's easy for me to hurt when others hurt. I'm one of the bleeding-heart, overly sentimental types for which the Christian Right has so little temperance. But I have to admit that in far too many instances the caring part of me tends to become subsumed by the self-defined importance of my own affairs. Sometimes I think too much about my own seemingly monolithic problems. I put me first, far too often, and I forget the far worse plight of others.

I forget that three-quarters of the world's population live in hunger and poverty.

I forget that too many of our children are abused and neglected.

I forget that families are torn apart by war and terrorism over which they have no control.

I forget that minorities are oppressed and discriminated against simply because of the color of their skin, or because they are from another culture, another country, or of another religion—and we don't even try to understand.

I forget that people die in the name of Christianity, or Islam, or Judaism, or any one of a score other theologies—all because we're too obstinate, too hate-filled, too narrow, and too petty to remember that the religions for which we kill are supposedly the crux of our life rooted in love.

I forget that women continue to be raped and beaten, and treated like second-class citizens—and we turn our backs and call it a domestic problem.

I forget that what was once the beautiful American dream has become for many a nightmare of crime and violence, drug, chemical, and alcohol dependency, divorce, suicide, and emotional turmoil.

I forget that our love of money has taught us how to cheat more efficiently, how to steal more proficiently, and how to rob each other of the human dignity we all deserve.

I forget that while we pray for peace, we continue to build weapons with which to kill.

And I forget...

But it needn't be that way. We don't have to forget!

We can learn to care about each other, again. We can learn to love instead of hate, to comfort instead of ignore, to compliment instead of insult, and to care for rather than to take advantage of. It doesn't take a lot of old-fashioned, Bible Belt religion, we don't need an infusion of God-fearing, right-wing scripture as some would have us believe, and we don't, after all, need a Waiting-for-Godot miracle to happen. We have the power to change the aberrant ways of the world by the strength of our minds and the love of our hearts. Caring is the power we need to apply.

There's nothing mysterious about it. It doesn't take training. We don't have to go to school to learn about it. There aren't any secret recipes involved. And we certainly don't need it peddled to us by double-talking, self-righteous, right-wing Christian hypocrites. It's not a miracle we need. It's good old-fashioned common sense caring. That's all it will take.

Granted, for most of us, exercising the power of caring may necessitate major changes in the way we live. We'll have to revolutionize our way of thinking, reorganize our way of behaving, and restructure our way of prioritizing. We might have to abandon some of our selfish comforts; sacrifice in order to accomplish the common good. Probably, we will have to focus our attention upon community, rather than upon ourselves.

But we can do it; it is possible. We've proven that a hundred times before: after hurricanes, and floods, tsunamis and earthquakes, tornadoes and fires. But it always seems to take a disaster of horrific magnitude to get us moving, to put things in perspective, to undo the apathy.

Think about it. Our self-assumed problems aren't really that bad, are they? We can at least try to forget our own frustrations and attempt to make life better for everyone. What is it going to take? What will finally motivate change? What threat might finally stimulate action? The threatened elimination of the human species? The final maelstrom of Armageddon? By then it would be too late for change. There no longer would be a purpose for changing.

When will we truly start caring about and loving the guy next door, the woman down the street, the child on the other side of town, the people in the far reaches of the world? They've got problems too. Can't we do something to help them? After all, we're a strong nation, we're intelligent people, we've got the money, we consider ourselves the policemen of the world, and we like to think of ourselves as having the answer for everything.

It's time we abandoned our bloated, self-important image of ourselves, as a nation, and gave it a try. Maybe we can't turn things around. Maybe we've progressed beyond the point of no return. Maybe *The Day the Earth Stood Still* has finally arrived. But just maybe we can make a difference. Maybe we can embrace others as we embrace ourselves. Perhaps a redefinition of our place in the world will afford hope to the disenfranchised—and after all, isn't that what life is really all about—hope?

Twenty Eight
Spiritual Revolution

Not all revolution has to do with bombs and bullets, although such are the toys of war, and indeed are most frequently associated with the violent dissolution of governments. Street theater and the contemporary expression of media-planned civil disobedience do little to encourage lasting sociopolitical change, or to mobilize zealots to levels of heroic sacrifice. Repetitious demonstrations have questionable effect upon reversing the historic flow of status quo politics and conservative ideology. Rather, the only permanent way by which serious revolutionary change can be made—be it political, social, economic, or structural—is to initiate spiritual revolution from within the self, and to infect society with a revolution of philosophy. In fact, the future of the G/L/B/T liberation movement, and indeed the future of all humankind, rests with a revolution of personal spirituality and the acceptance of metaphysical change as the focus upon which individual—and communal—freedom exists.

Spiritual revolution, and the evolution of social philosophy that should follow naturally, won't be easy to effect. Spiritual change demands much from the individual—and the community—by way of exorcising existing beliefs and rejecting secular comfort, and the realities of discomfort frequently dissuade the meek from embracing serious change. Those concerned with physical revolution see spirituality as being too

visionary and unrealistic, and those consumed with the political
are blinded by tunnel vision and short-term satisfaction.

Street-radicals, while milking the system for all the luxury
and civility they can, attempt to convince us that lasting
sociopolitical change can be accomplished by rhetorical illogic.
They rewrite history, lip-synch radical ideology, and play the
game of weekend radical, all the while reaping the harvest of a
system they say they consider corrupt and decadent.

More conservative revolutionaries (meaning those who want
change as long as it doesn't affect them adversely) insist that
buying into the system is acceptable, as long as you're on the
mailing list of at least one political action committee, while
benefiting from the more acceptable aspects of an otherwise
corrupt system. They quietly donate large sums of money to
politically correct organizations (from the privacy and protection
of the closet), attend gala affairs that raise money in a never-
ending cycle of self-serving egocentricity, and work for change
within the system.

Every liberation movement has developed its own toys of
revolution, from the indiscriminate tossing of bombs and
explosive rhetoric, to an insistence upon self-indulgent ideology
and the compromising of serious change for self-serving reward.
And yet, the permanence of revolution does not rest with
throwing bricks and bombs, marching in endless parades,
writing letters to deaf politicians, phone banking, vote counting,
media scrutiny, or rhetorical confusion. Although all of these
methods are necessary and have a legitimate place in the scheme
of revolution, they do not address the essence of change. They
are merely bandages applied to festering wounds. Real
revolution demands a rebirth of personal spirituality, which
ultimately translates into community reawakening.

As important as political activism is—and indeed, no
liberation movement could exist in a vacuum of secular
ignorance—political manipulation does not address the urgent
need for gay and lesbian spiritual revolution. Few of us would
challenge the need for changed laws, more responsive courts,
and a more tolerant society; but many of us balk at the idea of
committing self and community to spiritual revolution. It sounds

far too threatening to the status quo, and too unnerving concerning how we regard ourselves theologically.

It won't be legislation that will eventually define us as a people. It won't be the blind acceptance of social expectations that will afford us equal treatment under the law. It won't be a miraculous epiphany of the spirit that will win liberation with our churches and social institutions. Rather, it will be the liberation of self that moves us from being regarded as social pariahs, to being accepted as equal, productive members of this, or any, society.

The obscenity of racism still permeates America (and the world). Sexism, homophobia, xenophobia, ethnocentrism, and religious fundamentalism continue to stunt sociopolitical evolution. Despite the efforts of well-meaning crusaders, children and women are still being abused; there are still the hungry and homeless among us; disease and the threat of pandemic virus still go unchecked; our streets are unsafe to walk; crime is rampant; cynicism is abundant; malaise is spreading like disease—apathy and fear reign supreme.

We sit by and watch young black men kill other young black men. We turn a deaf ear to the suffering of unwanted children and poverty-entrenched single mothers. We ignore the pleas of the sick and the dying. We watch religions persecute in the name of God. We allow governments to discriminate. Our televisions flicker through dinner with images of crazed humans beating one another to death in the name of nationalistic pride. And we do little to address these problems other than to organize a symposium, toss a few coins at the problems, produce a television movie-of-the-week about the most current social issue, or sponsor a special month long celebration for the social/medical/racial/ethnic topic of the moment.

And we continue to die.

We need conservative organizations to work within the system and there is obviously a demand for radical groups to work the streets in outrage! We must cultivate the money of those who give, but withhold involvement. To effect serious change, however, to reverse the tide of mediocrity that eschews the evolution of human history, we must look deeply inward to the self and effect radical, permanent, and complete spiritual regeneration: a regeneration that goes beyond the definitions of contemporary religion, a regeneration that extends beyond the understanding of theology as we think it to be, a regeneration that goes to the heart and soul and mind of each of us as individuals—inexorably linked, not only to the world in which we live, but to the universe of which we are an integral part.

Spiritual regeneration isn't easy; most people shy away from significant change, fearing the ramifications of altering their way of life. To evolve from within means to shed from without— like the caterpillar that transforms into a butterfly. Still, if we ever hope to enact revolution that truly addresses and amends the way we live and the mess we've gotten ourselves into, the only manner by which we can adopt transformation is through personal, unequivocal spiritual regeneration.

At the heart of any social movement is the person who believes in herself and who can look inward with courage, confidence, and determination. At the core of who we are as gay men and lesbians is the self-understanding of emotional, spiritual, and cosmic health that all of us must achieve in order to prosper in a world that too often seems out of sync. In order to accomplish these self-altering truths, we must address several common realities in order to reach that pinnacle of self-understanding and self-acceptance that leads to unquestionable success.

First, we must accept who we are, and come out of our dark and lonely closets into the sunlight of personal liberation. The many years of pain we experience as closet-dwellers encourages self-hatred, self-deceit, and self-imposed alienation from family, friends, and society. The more we come out—individually and collectively—the stronger we become and the more the rest of the world realizes that, indeed, gays and lesbians are everywhere!

It is emotionally devastating to individual self-worth to believe the lies we have heard about ourselves all our lives: lies controlled by our churches, our courts, our schools, our peers, our government, and—too often—our own families. It is easy to shy away from a healthy acceptance of personal sexuality and live in a world of hypocrisy and deceit. And yet, that is what we do. We drown ourselves in liquor, drugs, and sex, hoping that one more drink, one more call, one more anonymous sexual encounter will lead to the happiness we so desperately seek. But they never do. The answers for which we search are not found in the bottom of a bottle, or under the sheets, but in our own self-understanding and our own personal honesty.

Second, we must demonstrate courage in the face of adversity. Discrimination and prejudice run rampant in our society; being gay or lesbian is not easy. And yet we dare not use fear as an excuse to shrink back into our closets of isolation; we must always be strong, proud, and courageous.

Courage marks the delineation between spiritual strength and weakness; not between physical power and cowardice. We all remember the plight of the Cowardly Lion from *The Wizard of Oz*. Not until the powerful wizard had tapped into the lion's inner strength did the lion believe that he possessed the qualities of courage. But his was not a lack of courage because of physical limitations—a lion is hardly a cowardly animal—but rather, because he did not understand that courage comes from within and not from intimidation, control, or the false adulation of those impressed by strength.

Howard Nemerov, in his poem "Life Cycle of the Common Man" writes: "Consider all the courage in living / and behold the man walking into deep silence...borne along on the breath which is his spirit / telling the numberless tale of his word / which makes the world his apple, and causes him to eat."

As gay men and lesbians we are no different from the lion in *The Wizard of Oz*, or from the common man in Nemerov's poem. We must summon our strength, look inward to those qualities that define us as individuals, and walk into the hostile silence...forcing the world to take notice and us to eat.

Third, we must accept individual responsibility and develop a sense of self-confidence that elevates us beyond the ordinary and into a world of unbounded faith. By coming out of the closet, by developing the courage necessary to survive in a world so often willing to hate, and by evolving a sense of self-confidence that accentuates the positive, we can create a wholeness of self-being that negates failure and emphasizes success.

Research into that elusive human characteristic called self-confidence has repeatedly demonstrated that positive self-esteem and a healthy sense of self-worth are the foundations upon which

we establish our sense of belonging in society, and from which
our very concept of individuality evolves. Without self-
confidence, we can be too easily defeated. Without self-
confidence, we see ourselves as weak, socially impotent, and
spiritually dead. Without self-confidence, we see ourselves as
corporeal anomalies who reflect unattractive physical qualities,
rather than as the beautiful people we are. Self-confidence is
paramount to a healthy understanding of self-worth and
individual success. Without it, there is little hope for personal
liberation; without it, there is an even less likelihood of
community survival.

Fourth, we must mature as confident individuals. We must
accept who we are, understand our possibilities and our
limitations, and develop a personal sense of self- acceptance. We
can love no one until we love our selves. We cannot hope to
achieve victory for the community until we achieve victory as
individuals. Lovers and friends should not and cannot
complete—they should complement. We must look inward to our
own courage and confidence and become personally motivated,
such that our strength and confidence flow through us and into
others in a flood of self-respect, self-determination, and self-
understanding.

And finally, we must achieve spiritual revelation through
religious experience or through universal awareness. For years,
psychologists have recognized the importance of spirituality—
our emotional and psychological health depends upon it. Indeed,
our struggle for equality demands that we confront issues of
legislative and judicial concern, but we dare not ignore the
importance of spirituality—a force that possesses the potential to
bring us together as a community and to anchor us as
individuals.

For much of our recent history, many gays and lesbians have
ignored spirituality, yet it is at the very core of our history and
subcultural heritage. Dare we forget the ancient shamans who
first gave rise to an understanding of homosexuality as a
spiritual gift that extended beyond the ordinary? Dare we ignore
the goddesses of our forbears who blessed us with an ethereal
understanding of truth beyond the secular? Dare we disregard
native spiritualists who honored homosexuality as a unique and

privileged third sex of man/woman? Dare we neglect the fairies, nymphs, and specters that created a mythology of our own? Dare we ignore the gods of all religions to whom we pay lip service, but little recognition? There is scant hope for the survival of a people who ignore history, who separate from their past, and who sunder from their spiritual connections.

We should not forget that all great liberation movements have been rooted in the forces of spirituality, but that does not suggest that we should embrace the doctrines that deceive us, nor adopt the religions that condemn us. Instead, we must accept our place in the universe—individually and collectively—as inhabitants of an experience that reaches far beyond our petty irritabilities and secular trivialities.

We must broaden our focus to include, not only the larger community of which we are a part, but the very cosmos to which we belong. We are not only gay men and lesbians, but individuals, undeniably linked in a continuum of history, evolution, and cosmic being. I am as much a part of you as you are of me; and we are all as much a part of community, and nation, and universe as they are a part of us.

We must rise above the discrimination, the hatred, and the prejudice that we experience as gay men and lesbians to embrace a philosophy that includes acceptance of all people regardless of race, status, religion, nationality, ethnic background, or any secular division that encourages separation.

The gay and lesbian equality movement has the potential and the opportunity to extend far beyond the simplistic concept of tunnel-vision liberation and explode into a universal reality that demands the liberation of people, everywhere. Seldom has a group of people been so hated. Seldom has a group of people been so challenged. And seldom has a group of people had the opportunity to extend beyond the dreams of today, and reach for the possibilities of tomorrow.

But, it can only happen if we are willing to accept ourselves as loving, good, and successful people.

It can only happen if we are willing to develop a sense of self-worth and self-understanding.

It can only happen if we accept our spiritual nature. And it can only happen if we learn to unequivocally and completely love one another, as gays, as lesbians, as friends, as family—as one people—one children of the universe.

Twenty Nine
11:59:59 Old / 12:00:00 New

New Year's Eve is a curious time of year, a holiday juxtaposed with celebration and regret, contemplation and dream, remembrance and anticipation. Most of us are relieved to see the old year pass and more than happy to usher in a new one filled with the promise of a fresh beginning. It has become a time synonymous with personal reflection and determined resolve: reflection upon that which we have, or have not accomplished and resolution to do better under new and different circumstances.

We make decisions, rue the passing of time, and wish away problems—hoping they will magically disappear as the clock changes from 11:59:59 PM on December 31 of any year to 12:00:00 midnight of a sparkling new January 1. And we repeat the whole scenario year after endless year, confidently reassuring ourselves that the flipping of a calendar page will trigger a long-awaited transformation of personal habits and luck.

Of course, in practical terms, New Year's Eve really doesn't mean all that much. It is merely symbolic—a ritualization of death and resurrection facilitated by a ceremonial evocation of the rites of passage. We think of New Year's Eve as a time for cleansing—a midwinter's spring-cleaning of the mind and soul that becomes the embodiment of our desire to start fresh. Out with the old, in with the new!

Certainly, there is something to be said for symbolism and ritual, especially on New Year's Eve. They allow us the opportunity to purge ourselves of that which is bad and actuate that which is good. But we engage symbolism and ritual everyday of our lives, not just on New Year's Eve. Whether it is as superstition and fable, religion and philosophy, or pageant and theater, symbolism and ritual have become embedded in the cultural mythology that dictates our norms, taboos, and social expectations.

Ritual helps mark the various passages of life. Symbolism assists in focusing upon change. Both provide the security and continuity for which we long in an otherwise hostile and chaotic world. Humankind has marked virtually every significant passage of one stage of life to another with ritual and ceremony—from circumcision to rites of passage into man (and woman) hood, to graduation from school, to marriage, and even to death.

We humans are conditioned into thinking in terms of significant passage, so we create ritual to denote important changes in our lives. For each change we invent another ritual, and although we accept change as an inevitable part of living, we fear that which it entails; that which it demands, for change means that things with which we are familiar (and comfortable) will somehow be altered and life will never be the same, again.

It means there will be changes in the way we live and modifications in the manner by which we do things. It means we've closed one chapter of life and opened another, and that can be down right scary for anyone. So, we create rites of passage— rituals and symbols—simply to make us feel better and to help calm the fear of change. It is curious that we emphasize one single evening and two meaningless seconds as the determining factors when passing from one part of life into another. We usually neglect change during the rest of the year—we don't make resolutions during July and we seldom attempt to change bad habits in October.

Generally, we seem satisfied to stumble through life, half-asleep, until New Year's Eve when we feel compelled, or obligated, into making promises and plans we have little intention of keeping.

Change should be regarded as an ever-evolving process. Few of us are comfortable with regarding life as being in a state of constant flux—but it is! We make changes almost daily. We leave jobs and start new ones, end love affairs and begin different ones, bury our dead and celebrate birth, make decisions, violate promises, grow older, become wiser; and laugh, and cry, and—change.

New Year's Eve is convenient. It marks a physical passage of time from one numerical denotation to the next, so it becomes easy for us to embellish it with symbolism and ritual and to think of it in terms of being the first day of the rest of our lives.

Of course, it's perfectly acceptable to think of January 1 as the first day of the rest of our lives—in some respects it is, but no more so than any other day might be. If, however, a new calendar year makes facilitating change easier, let us use it. And if such be the case, then resolutions are in order. Promises are necessary, and behavioral transformation is beneficial. But, it is critical to stick with our decisions and not give up after one ill-fated month of trying, because, if, indeed, January 1 does symbolize personal transformation, then it should become something more than just vacant symbolism.

Life is ever changing—always evolving; so January 1st and all the other firsts and days between should become the first days of the rest of our lives.

Ritual is good when used for specific purposes; symbolism is necessary in order to understand change, but it is important to accept that change is more than just empty tradition obscured by a frivolous holiday of champagne and "Auld Lang Syne." New Year's Eve should be a time for personal reflection. If it is to afford the opportunity for change, then, indeed, it must be approached as if it truly were the first day of the rest of our lives.

Thirty
The Mirror

Where do you go from here, when here is anywhere you want it to be, or would like it to be, and if you could have it be where ever you wanted it to be—just where would you go?

You're middle-aged and mildly successful in your career. You have never screwed up seriously; in fact you've been relatively proficient in most things you've attempted. Supervisors at work have always complimented you, coworkers admire you, acquaintances and peers respect you, and you've accomplished much of what you initially set out to do—a long time ago.

Love has been typical, more so than some, less than others. You've loved and lost—like everyone else—so there isn't anything you can really grumble about concerning romance. You have memories of warm summer days and chilly autumn nights and a hundred other thoughts of being together with that special person who kept you satisfied in your long winter of discontent.

You have a nice place to live—a small house though it might be—and even though you complain about not having the glamorous surroundings so many of the people your age seem to have, you know that your accommodations are palatial compared to most of the world's population, and so you accept your abode without an excessive amount of protest. You've got a car—not paid off, of course—but at least it's transportation, and like most Americans, you're up to your neck in debt. Your home is filled with the knickknacks that typify your unique clutter, such as used furniture, books, a stereo with CDs, tons of out-dated and unused LPs, newer DVDs, and a thousand and one memories that you've been given or have collected over the years. You've got all the things that you want, but you keep thinking that you really don't seem to have anything at all, and you keep wondering where do you go from here?

It seems that one gloomy January morning you awoke, stumbled into the bathroom to attend to all of those 6:00 a.m. routines that have become ritual, and looked into the mirror.

The mirror!

That impartial reminder of mortality that greets you every morning with regularity and without comment—until that one morning when it's more than you care to accept. And you look into that mirror of truth and wonder who is staring back at you.

It can't be you! You're only twenty-one and fresh-faced. There shouldn't be any age lines creasing your forehead. There shouldn't be any bags sagging under you eyes. There shouldn't be crow's-feet marring your skin. There shouldn't be receding hair on your scalp, or gray tinting the edges of your once-upon-a-time brown. There shouldn't be weariness in your smile, or a stoop to your posture. That isn't you. It can't be. You aren't old! An impostor has laid claim to your mirror!

The mirror—that trickster of honesty has betrayed you! Mirror, mirror on the wall, who's the fairest...damn, you don't even need to finish that hackneyed old fairy tale. You aren't the fairest of them all—any more. The years have slipped by without your noticing. Suddenly, seemingly overnight, you've morphed into someone you don't recognize; you aren't that pimply-skinned kid any longer. Unexpectedly, as though you had blundered into some bizarre Star Trek time warp, you've aged beyond late-night parties, three hours of sleep, and believing that Christmas won't come for a long, long time.

The mirror—that fickle demon of candor has wrenched your youth out from under your nose, and gradually replaced every thought of tomorrow with memories from yesterday. The dreams and goals and aspirations that had been the bastion upon which you built your future, have crumbled into a reality of midlife that, upon first glance, seems common...ordinary...unacceptable.

You have become your own most terrifying nightmare! The mirror—that inanimate object that cannot support your sagging ego, dares reflect back a truth you prefer not to accept. You are not twenty-something any more. You are not eagerly embarking upon a journey that will lead to unequivocal success. You cannot think in terms of youthful forever; the days ahead are fewer than the ones behind.

The mirror—that deceitful bearer of the truth. You'd break it if...if...if it didn't mean seven years bad luck. Can you afford seven years of any kind of luck? Do you even have seven years left? According to the mirror, you've aged well beyond what you had ever thought you'd become. You are forced into remembering back to a time when even thirty seemed old and ponderous. Now you're well beyond that, and that damn mirror won't allay, change, or nullify the memories of people and places and times that existed in your life long before you became what you now see in its depth. Those memories really are just that and there isn't a darn thing you can do to alter where you've been, or where you've ended up.

The mirror—if only you could change into Dorian Gray, with all the wear and tear of your face and body transmuted to a painting in the attic. Or maybe you could embark on a search for the Fountain of Youth, but not like poor old Ponce de Leon whose quest ultimately led him to madness. Perhaps you could close your eyes and repeat over and over again that you believe, you believe—and Peter Pan would appear out of nowhere.

But those are imaginings, stories, make believe, while the mirror is reality. You aren't Dorian Gray, or Ponce de Leon, or Peter Pan, or any one of a hundred other whimsical fantasies or mythologies about lost youth. You are who you are—age lines, aching joints, and restless thoughts—and what you have as your witness is...the mirror.

The mirror, the reflection of the physical that exists on the outside, somehow makes you feel that what is left on the inside is less than what you had hoped for. So you stare intently, change positions, look more deeply, and gaze again upon that which looks back out at you. You take a deep breath, decide that this is a horror from which you will awaken and eagerly await that magical moment that will miraculously transport you back to a spring morning and a bright-eyed youth who has ten thousand days stretching out ahead.

Upon closer examination, you realize that it is you staring back from deep within the frankness of that mirror. Age lines crease your brow, but the face is vaguely familiar. Your hair has, indeed, receded and is grayer than it was several years ago, but that smile is faintly similar. Your stoop is noticeable, your shoulder aches from sleeping on the wrong side last night, and your teeth aren't as Hollywood gleaming as they were when you were young. But it is you, of that you are certain. You cannot escape that older age has laid claim to your once-upon-a-time youth. Somehow, somewhere along the way, while you were busy with the realities of work, life, and growing older that face gaping back at you from within the mirror (or is it from within yourself?), became you! And out of the blue, one chilly winter morning you innocently gaze into your bathroom mirror and see who you have become, and you wonder:

Where do I go from here?

Appendix

This is a speech that was delivered to an organization called Your Forefront, an educational organization that promotes diversity. It was presented by the author at the Stanley A. Aranoff Center for the Performing Arts in Cincinnati, Ohio on Saturday, February 25, 2006.

The Worst of Times, But Your Best of Times

Charles Dickens once wrote: *It was the best of times and it was the worst of times,* and indeed, we are living in an era that is both the best and the worst of times. One only need look at the current political situation, the myriad of state legislatures around the country violating gay rights, citizen referenda voting to constitutionalize bigotry and inequality, and the raging debate concerning gay marriage to understand that in many respects it is the worst of times. On the other hand, one need only consider television programming like the hit show *Will and Grace*, the currently popular movie *Brokeback Mountain*, or the more open acceptance of homosexuality by the younger generation to realize that in other respects, it is the best of times. Certainly, the times in which we now live are characterized by a dichotomy of attitudes: a more tolerant acceptance of homosexuality by a slim majority of Americans, but still, a political and religious intolerance that embraces right-wing conservatism as though it were the basis upon which this nation should endure. Well, it is not! Despite what pontificating politicians and holier-than-thou homophobes might have you believe, this nation still portends the greatest hope for humankind—and that includes gay, lesbians, bisexuals, and transgendered people. This nation is comprised of a more tolerant and accepting people than many would have us think and, quite honestly, in the past ten years we have become a citizenry—especially the younger generation—built upon the very concepts of acceptance that social extremists so very much hate.

Take a look around. It is not unusual, today, to witness heterosexual teenage boys mimicking the dress, the styles, the language, and in some instances, even the behavior of their gay peers. Earrings, that are so popular with younger straight men, were originally the province of queers. Baggy pants and streaked hair were made popular by fags. Much of the slang words and expressions used by younger people, today, are antiquated euphemisms popularized by homosexual men in an attempt to communicate with one another, but to hide their sexuality from the majority community. But it wasn't so long ago that being overtly queer constituted an open invitation to verbal harassment at the best, and physical bashing at the worst. Again, the best and the worst of times.

And yet, as I address you tonight, those of us in this room are, in many instances, the lucky ones. Although I don't know where each of you comes from, or what your individual circumstances might be, we are fortunate to live in a metropolitan area, that—even though conservative and reactionary—is a far better lot than living in rural America where fag bating and bashing are still a way of life. Imagine an event of this size being held in Nowhereville, Ohio or Smallburg, Kentucky or Littletown, Anywhere. It just wouldn't happen. We wouldn't have had eaten at a popular downtown restaurant, we wouldn't be meeting in one of the largest performance centers in the city, and we wouldn't have gay and lesbian organizations to give us guidance, a chance to be open, and an opportunity to express ourselves as we are. We are lucky to be living in one of the best of places, although it isn't perfect.

I know some of you might be thinking: *Great...that's all well and good, but tell us something we don't know. Tell us something*

we can relate to, something we can embrace for our generation.
Some of you might even be thinking: *Who does this old guy think
he is? How can he possibly understand what I'm going through,
how I feel, what my circumstances are?* OK, I'll grant you the fact
that I don't know what it is like to be a teenaged gay or lesbian
in 2006 America. I can't assume that I understand your exact
circumstances, your family situations, your friendship circles, or
at the very least, what might be filtering through your mind day
in and day out. But I can stand before you and tell you I know
what it is like growing up gay during a time when a gay man or
a lesbian didn't even dare utter the word queer, let alone act on
an impulse, a thought, or an action without taking the chance of
being physically attacked, or even killed. And I can let you know
that no matter how dire your personal situation might seem,
there are people who care about you, who love you, and who have
been fighting for decades to make this world a better place for
you.

That's why I'm here tonight: to let you know that there are
only a few simple truths to being gay that can assure you of a life
filled with happiness, self-enlightenment, confidence, and self-
respect. And those few simple truths are so close to you right
now that you could—at this very moment—make the decision to
reach out, pluck them from the branch of liberation, and free
yourself to live as you are intended to live.

Politically, this might very well be some of the worst of times,
but you have the choice, you have the control, you have the
opportunity to make these days and the rest of the days ahead of
you—the very best of times.

It isn't easy growing up being a gay or lesbian young person.
Almost everything you hear about homosexuality is shrouded in
prejudice and misunderstanding:

- The church claims it is a sin
- Cities and states legislate against it
- Parents usually ignore the whole subject, or worse—
direct you towards every heterosexual path imaginable
- The schools banish information about homosexuality
from the curriculum
- For the most part, Hollywood and television portray gays

and lesbians as swishy fems, butch dykes, and scandalous ne'er-do-wells

• Our friends tell fag jokes—and we tell fag jokes—and then die a little more inside each time we laugh, knowing full well that, all the while, we're ridiculing ourselves.

Everything we hear or see about homosexuality is linked to negative images; there isn't anything positive about being queer—it isn't the All American way to be.

Society will try to convince you that you're somehow unnatural. The church might claim to love you out of one side of its mouth, but out of the other side, will condemn your sin. Politicians will pontificate about the sanctity of holy matrimony, but deny you the right to live in spousal union with the person you love. In some cases family will disown you, friends will abandon you, teachers will ignore (or even ridicule) you, and during the darkest days of your self-doubt, you will be coerced into learning how to hate yourself.

But it needn't be that way. This world is replete with rules and regulations and dogma that makes little sense—created by humans. My philosophy has always been: take what you want and damn the rest. Don't be afraid to be who you are, because through it all, and in the end—at the very end of this experience we call life—you have only yourself to whom you must answer. And that is why those simple truths I mentioned earlier are so critical to your existence. They are the difference between simply living, and being happy!

That's why coming out of your closet is so critical! Certainly as a community—but more importantly, as the young people you are—you must come out emotionally, physically, and spiritually. As long as there are just the few fighting for the rights of the many, no one—politician, religious leader, housewife, or corporate executive—will believe that there are as many of us as there are. Only when society realizes that we are their teachers, their ministers, their bankers, their truck drivers, their plumbers, their politicians, their ball players, and—YES—their children, will we begin to win the battle for equality and self-respect.

Coming out of the closet means verbally acknowledging your queer orientation to those who immediately surround you and are important to you. It means telling your parents and siblings, your closest friends, and the other people whom you identify as being significant in your life. Certainly, each individual has to decide who among your sphere of influence needs to know—no one can determine that for you. Coming out means facing yourself, acknowledging your sexual identity and living your life in the open air of singularity—not continuing to live a life of duplicity and lies.

Coming out isn't easy. By coming out you risk losing your family, being abandoned by your friends, and indeed, sacrificing your very safety. But remaining hidden in the closet is far worse psychologically and emotionally for anyone; it promises nothing but a continuum of deceit, self-recrimination, doubt, and self-hatred.

Coming out means shouting from the rooftops that you're queer and being proud of who you are. It means realizing that every day for the rest of your life you will have to come out again and again every time you meet someone new, every time you become involved in a new situation, every time you move to a new school, or begin a new job. It means facing the reality that the process of coming out is one that lasts a lifetime—it isn't a simple decision that is implemented one day and then forgotten about the next. Coming out means living your life honestly—and openly—from that point forward.

Coming out is unique to people in the G/L/B/T community because, for the most part, the rest of the world doesn't know us for who we truly are. We don't necessarily look, walk, talk, or dress gay (well...not all the time, anyway!); we aren't easy to identify like other minorities. For us gays and lesbians, there just aren't any distinguishing physical, psychological, or emotional characteristics that uniquely indicate our sexual orientation.

I've been asked by sincerely interested heterosexuals: *So what's the big deal, why do you have to come out, what's so important about announcing your sexual orientation to the world? We don't! Can't you just be quiet about it and still be who you are?*

In a few words...NO...absolutely not. We will not be coerced into hiding our sexual identity simply because it makes some straight man or woman more comfortable. We will not be quiet about being queer when we are discriminated against and are denied the same civil rights that heterosexuals enjoy. We will not be quiet about being gay when we continue to be harassed and beaten and become the uncounted victims of hate crimes! We will not be quiet about our orientation when we are denied jobs and housing and equal opportunity. We will not be quiet about who we are when we are denied the right to marry or join in civil unions. And we will not be quiet about being a fag or a dyke when we continue to be the butt of jokes that spill from the mouths of narrow-minded hypocrites and bigots. And why should we be quiet? Why shouldn't we be proud of who and what we are? We have the same right to equality guaranteed by the Constitution of the United States as does anyone else. As far as heterosexuals not having to announce their sexual orientation, well of course not. The overwhelming percentage of the world's population is heterosexual, why should straight people have to go around announcing anything about their sexuality? Everything in this country—from the laws that govern us, to the social mores to which we are expected to conform, to expectations of our life-course—is geared towards being heterosexual. Obviously straight people don't have to come out—sexual identity is inherent to being heterosexual!

But coming out doesn't mean providing people with every detail about your life, or personal proclivities—such is information to be shared only by the most intimate of friends. The entire world should not be privy to information that is neither appropriate to their understanding, nor is any of their business. But it does mean being honest—to the rest of the world and to yourself—politically, intellectually, socially, and spiritually. The decision to come out is, certainly, one of individual choice—one that can only be made by each of you depending upon individual circumstances. None of us can tell another gay or lesbian when he or she should come out. But I wonder when will we cease being ashamed of ourselves and accept that we are valuable and equal members of this (or any) society? When will we stop making excuses for whom and what we are? When will we stand up and fight for that piece of the American Pie that we were told about and promised as children?

Does our struggle demand individual bravery and self-sacrifice? Absolutely. The success of any liberation movement is built upon the backs of those who sacrificed for the common good, and individual sacrifice is legitimate bravery.

Coming out as a gay man, a lesbian, a bisexual, or transgendered means far more than a quickie in your friend's bedroom, and then slithering back into the closet before someone finds out. Coming out means more than acting the part when you're with one of your queer friends, then returning to hetero-mimicry when you're with straight people. Coming out means more than paying lip service to the cause of liberation and the honor of self-dignity. Coming out means more than playing at being gay or lesbian, then steadfastly denying (by word or silence) your sexuality to family, friends, teachers, and employers. Coming out means more than simply sneaking off to a one-time-a-year pride event, then slinking back into the shadows of deceit.

Coming out means being yourself, establishing networks of friends who share your sexual orientation, trusting teachers and other caring adults who empathize with the plight society has forced upon you. Coming out means throwing open the doors of your dark and lonely closet and rushing headlong into the sunlight of self-enlightenment. Coming out means developing confidence in who you are, what you want out of life, and directing all of your energy towards living openly, honestly, and with pride.

I have been asked, from time to time, by well-intentioned gays what is so important about coming out. I have been asked by them—much as I have been by straight people—*why can't we just be who we are in silence; after all, isn't becoming a part of the majority society our goal?* Yes, incorporating into the majority is one of our goals, but as long as we remain in our closets, as long as we assume that our sexual identity doesn't make a difference, as long as we assume that some sympathetic heterosexual politician will come along one day and hand us equality on a silver platter, then we are in for a long and difficult struggle. It is important that everyone we know—from family, to friends, to classmates, to acquaintances—knows who and what we are. With numbers comes liberation.

You can take a giant step toward personal integrity, pride, and universal equality by taking that one step out of the closet, accepting who you are, and demanding that the lies that encase us in a tomb of defeat cease—immediately and once and for all!

And yet, even with personal acceptance achieved, sometimes we still end up, if only for a fleeting moment, feeling a little depressed and a bit disconnected from the world around us. We will dislike ourselves again and begin to feel ill at ease with who and what we are. That's not unusual, it's not hypocritical, and it's not our fault. It happens to every gay man and lesbian at one time or another. After all, being queer means constantly living with the realization that we are not like the majority of the world. Being queer invariably means fighting for our very souls. Being queer means undoing all those years of forced, negative conditioning. Being queer means reprogramming everything that was imprinted in our minds at an early age. But during those times of deepest despair, it is critical to remember that we are good people, we are equal to anyone else, and we are entitled to live life as fully and with as much pleasure as we can.

Here I paraphrase, in part, Dorothy Parker's perspicacious wit:

> I was seventy-seven, come August,
> I shall shortly be losing my bloom,
> I've experienced zephyr and raw gust,
> And (symbolical) flood and simoom.
> When you come to this time of abatement,
> To this passing from Summer to Fall,
> I shall say (if my memory's faithful)
> I have no regret for it all.

And, like Ms. Parker, neither should you. Don't regret. Don't let this big beautiful world with so much promise and happiness pass you by. Come out. Be strong. Be confident. And live the life that makes you the unique person you are.

Endnotes

[1]A hunk is a gay man who is exceptionally good looking, well built, strong in physical appearance, and muscular (this term is no different than the same one used in the heterosexual community).

[2]A stud is similar to a hunk, except a stud is perceived as being more sexually active, promiscuous, and willing to engage in sex on a moment's notice. In common parlance the term stud, as applied to men, evolved from a stud horse that is used to sire physically well-bred offspring (this term is no different than the same word used in the heterosexual community).

[3]A daddy is usually an older gay man who befriends a younger man in a mutual exchange of services. The daddy provides money and/or gifts, in exchange for sexual favors from the younger man. A daddy need not always be an older gay man; often, the mutual exchange of services is affected between men of similar age, but of differing psychological manifestations (the daddy being more commanding and confident; whereas the younger gay man is usually less confident and is looking for security and attention). The term is sometimes also used in connection with sado-masochistic practices.

[4]A bear is a gay man, often an older man, with an abundance of facial and body hair. In some situations, a bear is also overweight in addition to being hairy. It is not unusual for bears to not only be attracted to other bears, but to younger, smooth-skinned twinks (see endnote [5]).

⁵A twink is a young gay man, usually between the ages of 21 and 28 (the age range differs depending upon whom one consults), who is usually considered physically attractive, not terribly intelligent (or acts in that way), and manifests behavior that includes teasing (suggesting the exchange of sexual intimacy, but withholding his part of the "tease" when he is confronted), cruising (moving about a gay bar or event in search of a sexual hook-up), and strutting (the act of walking in a manner that suggests sexuality and showmanship).

⁶Abraham Maslow (1908-1970), a noted psychologist, developed the Maslow Hierarchy of Needs scale that established the levels of personal actuation that he believed all people need to attain on their journey through life. His theory established a psychological hierarchy that led to the fulfillment of the individual. Maslow's hierarchy begins with the most basic of human needs: food, water, shelter, and safety, and progresses up the scale through the need for companionship, belonging, and self-awareness, and eventually to the pinnacle of success—the complete self-actualization of the individual, a level that few people ever achieve, except for fleeting times during their lives.

⁷Luigi Pirandello (1867-1936) was a Sicilian novelist and playwright. Though Pirandello wrote a number of novels and novellas, he is most famous for his plays, including *Naked Masks, Right You Are (If You Think You Are), To Clothe the Naked, The Life I Gave You, and Six Characters in Search of an Author.* The analysis and dissolution of a unified self are carried to an extreme in *Sei personaggi in cerca d'autore* (1921) [*Six Characters in Search of an Author*] where the stage itself, the symbol of appearance versus reality, becomes the setting of the play.

⁸Alfred Adler (1870-1937) was an Austrian psychologist and founder of the school of individual psychology. Although Adler was one of Sigmund Freud's early associates, he ultimately rejected Freudian emphasis upon sex as the root of neurosis. His major theory presumed that helplessness during childhood led to an inferiority complex, which he believed could be overcome through positive social interaction.

⁹Carl Gustav Jung (1875-1961) practiced a unique and broadly influential approach to psychology that emphasized

understanding the psyche through exploring the worlds of dreams, art, mythology, world religion and philosophy. He is probably the most well known pioneer in the field of dream analysis. He spent a great deal of his life's work exploring Eastern vs. Western philosophy, alchemy, astrology, sociology, literature, and the arts

[10]An A-gay is a gay man who is usually employed in a professional career (although not all the time), earns at least an upper-middle class salary, and is concerned with status, money, the accumulation of material goods, and prestige. The term A-gay is synonymous with another gay-slang term, Guppie, which is an altered spelling of the more commonly used and understood word Yuppie (upwardly mobile young person).

[11] A chicken is a young gay male, usually between the ages of 18 and 22 (depending upon the age of sexual consent in a particular state). The age of a chicken can, of course, vary depending upon one's perspective and age.

[12] A chicken hawk is an older gay man (age may vary depending upon one's perspective) who specifically searches for younger gay men (chicken) for sexual intimacy or emotional relationships.

[13] Dowager is a derivation of the traditional dowager widow who holds a title or property derived from her deceased husband; or an elderly woman of high social standing. In the gay community a dowager is an older man—usually past 50—who has significant standing in the gay community, but is not necessarily active in gay politics or the gay bar culture. A dowager is considered a "retired" gay activist, and by some younger gay men as being over-the-hill.

[14] Harvey Milk (1930-1978) was the first openly gay person to be elected to the Board of Supervisors of a large city, San Francisco (1977). Milk was a political activist in San Francisco before being elected to public office, and he was one of the earliest gay activists to insist on equality for homosexuals, not tolerance. On November 27, 1978 Milk and San Francisco mayor George Moscone, were assassinated by disgruntled former Supervisor Danny White. White's lawyer successfully argued what has now become known as the "Twinkie Defense," claiming that White could not be held accountable for his actions due to

the amount of junk food he had eaten on the day of the murders. White was found guilty of two counts of voluntary manslaughter, rather than murder. He was paroled after six years and committed suicide shortly thereafter. In an ironic twist of fate, Milk had tape-recorded several renditions of his political will which he labeled: "to be read in the event of my assassination." On one of the tapes he spoke the following: "If a bullet should enter my brain, let that be the bullet that destroys every closet door."

15 Frank Kameny (1925 –) was one of the early leaders of the gay rights movement and co-founder of the Washington, D.C. Mattachine Society, a homophile group that had started in Los Angeles ten years earlier. The name Mattachine comes from a French Renaissance folk dance that satirized the elite. The first meeting of the D.C. chapter, held on November 15, 1961, drew about twelve men and women. Kameny is considered one of the fathers of the gay rights movement and is still active today.

16 Henry "Harry" Hay (1913-2002) founded the country's first gay rights organization, The Mattachine Society, in Los Angeles, California, in 1950. The group operated largely underground. In the 1970s Harry Hay founded the gay men's spiritual group, the Radical Faeries. Hay was also the author of a collection of essays called, "Radically Gay: Gay Liberation in the Words of Its Founder." Considered by many to be the founder of the modern American gay rights movement, Hay never did embrace the concept of the more recent steps that have brought gays openly into the mainstream of society.

17 Alice B. Toklas (1877-1967) gained worldwide fame when her lover, Gertrude Stein, named her own biography, *The Autobiography of Alice B. Toklas* (1934). Both women lived as openly lesbian lovers in an era when being homosexual was virtually unheard of. After Stein's death in 1946, Toklas wrote her own book titled, *The Alice B. Toklas Cookbook* (1954), which made her famous for her recipe from artist Brion Gysin for hashish fudge, now more commonly known as Alice B. Toklas brownies.

18 Dorothy Parker (1903-1967) was a poet, humorist, short story writer, political activist, and member of the Algonquin Round Table—a group of New York writers. Parker is most

famous for her first collection of cynical poetry entitled *Enough Rope* which pontificated on women's issues including the loneliness of urban life, women's social roles, and female sexuality. She won the O. Henry award in 1929 for her short story "Big Blonde," a story about the tribulations of a "kept woman." Although married twice, Parker consistently defended the sexual liberation of women, which led many to believe she was a lesbian. Parker never acknowledged, publicly, whether or not she was. She continued her political activism throughout her life, notably organizing Hollywood screenwriters to a leftist cause, which resulted in her being blacklisted. Parker became a recluse later in her life and died of a heart attack, alone in her Manhattan hotel room in 1967.

www.ingramcontent.com/pod-product-compliance
Lightning Source LLC
Chambersburg PA
CBHW030012290326
41934CB00005B/304